The Spirit of the
BUDDHA

Martine Batchelor

AMARYLLIS

This editon first published 2011

AMARYLLIS

An imprint of Manjul Publishing House Pvt. Ltd.

Editorial Office:
J-39, Ground Floor, Jor Bagh Lane,
New Delhi 110 003, India
Tel: 011-24642447/24652447 Fax: 011-24622448
Email: amaryllis@amaryllis.co.in
Website: www.amaryllis.co.in

Registered Office:
10, Nishat Colony, Bhopal 462 003, M.P., India

ISBN: 978-81-910673-9-2

Printed and Bound in India by
Thomson Press (India) Limited

The Spirit of the
BUDDHA

Sacred Literature

The International Sacred Literature Trust was established to promote understanding and open discussion between and within faiths and to give voice in today's world to the wisdom that speaks across time and traditions.

What resources do the sacred traditions of the world possess to respond to the great global threats of poverty, war, ecological disaster, and spiritual despair?

Our starting-point is the sacred texts with their vision of a higher truth and their deep insights into the nature of humanity and the universe we inhabit. The publishing program is planned so that each faith community articulates its own teachings with the intention of enhancing its self-understanding as well as the understanding of those of other faiths and those of no faith.

The Trust especially encourages faiths to make available texts which are needed in translation for their own communities and also texts which are little known outside a particular tradition but which have the power to inspire, console, enlighten, and transform. These sources from the past become resources for the present and future when we make inspired use of them to guide us in shaping the contemporary world.

Our religious traditions are diverse but, as with the natural environment, we are discovering the global interdependence of human hearts and minds. The Trust invites all to participate in the modern experience of interfaith encounter and exchange which marks a new phase in the quest to discover our full humanity.

To
the memorists, scholars and translators
of ancient and present times

Contents

Acknowledgements

I would like to thank everyone at Yale University Press as well as at the International Sacred Literature Trust. It has been a pleasure to work with Malcolm Gerratt, my editor at ISLT. I am deeply grateful that the Buddhist Publication Society gave me permission to use quotes from *The Life of the Buddha* and that Wisdom Publications allowed me to quote from *The Numerical Discourses, The Long Discourses of the Buddha* and *The Middle Length Discourses of the Buddha*. I am indebted to Andrew Olendzki for letting me use his translation of the poem about the 'farmer' situated at the beginning of the book from the *Sutta Nipata*. I am grateful for the help of Ven. Bhikkhu Bodhi, Andrew Olendzki and Stephen Batchelor. Any errors are mine.

So you claim to be a farmer . . .
but we do not see you ploughing!
Tell me, since you've asked, of ploughing
so I'll know what you call 'ploughing'.

Faith is the seed, practice the rain,
and wisdom is my yoke and plough.
Modesty's the pole, mind the strap,
mindfulness my ploughshare and goad.

Body and speech are guarded well,
and food and drink have been restrained.
Truthfulness I use for weeding
and gentleness urges me on.

Effort is my beast of burden,
pulling me onward to safety.
On it goes without returning
where, having gone, one does not grieve

This is how I plough my ploughing –
the crop it yields is deathlessness!
And when one has ploughed this ploughing,
one is released from all suffering.

Sutta Nipata, I, 4

Introduction

In 1975, when I was twenty-two years old, I became a Zen nun in a Buddhist temple in South Korea. Since 1972 I had been living and working in London, where I became interested in Buddhism. I went to Tibetan Buddhist ceremonies, I read Zen books, and thought of doing Buddhist meditation. For this reason I decided to travel to Asia to find a meditative path.

I went to Nepal and India, where I did not have much opportunity to experience Buddhist teachings and practices because, as a first time traveller, I had secured the wrong visa and had to leave immediately. So I travelled to Thailand, where I met Buddhists monks and laypeople and started to meditate. But I was pulled towards Zen Buddhism and finally arrived in Korea, where I decided to become a Zen Buddhist nun.

After ten years, circumstances changed and I disrobed and gave back my nun's vows. I then married a British former Tibetan Buddhist Gelug monk and returned to Europe to live in a Buddhist community in Devon, England. Most members of that community were Theravada Buddhists from a modern Vipassana school that had originated in Burma. I participated in a few Vipassana retreats and found that the meditative techniques taught in these retreats were useful and effective. So I began to practise both Zen and Vipassana meditation.

I started to read books from different Buddhist teachers and traditions, and became more and more interested in early Buddhism and the original teachings of the Buddha as found in the Pali Canon. The book that inspired me the most and that I have read several times since was *The Life of the Buddha, as it appears in the Pali Canon*, as translated and edited by Bhikkhu Nanamoli. I was struck by how the Buddha came alive through the quotations from the Pali Canon judiciously chosen and organised by Bhikkhu Nanamoli.

In this text the Buddha appeared as a human being living in his own cultural conditions and trying to find a path to resolve his suffering and how to become a fully awakened person. By being able to achieve this not only did he benefit himself but he went on to teach and help others for forty-five years. When the opportunity came to write a book about the spirit of the Buddha, I decided that the best way to compose it, since I did not know Pali, was to use mainly quotations from *The Life of the Buddha, as it appears in the Pali Canon*, as Bhikkhu Nanamoli had already made an excellent choice and my task was to refine this choice for a contemporary audience of the twentieth-first century.

The 'Pali Canon' is a body of texts taught by the Buddha, which has been preserved in the Pali language. Pali is a form of popular Sanskrit also known as a 'prakrit'. Sanskrit was the language of the Brahmanical religion in India. For example, the *Upanishads* have been recorded in Sanskrit. Pali is to Sanskrit what Italian is to Latin. The Buddha did not speak Pali, but he might have spoken a number of Sanskrit-based dialects. Pali is a literary version of these Sanskrit-based dialects. Over time it became the lingua franca for Buddhist monks who lived in different regions of India, so that they had a common language in which they could recite and memorise the Buddha's teachings found in the suttas – discourses delivered by the Buddha or one of his prominent disciples.

The Pali Canon was recited and memorized communally by groups of monastics for three to four hundred years before it was inscribed on palm leaves in Sri Lanka. There is no Pali script as such. It is the tradition to transcribe the Pali Canon in the specific script of each country. The Pali Canon was first written down in Sinhalese. Since then it has been transcribed in Burmese and other East-Asian scripts, and nowadays Westerners can read the Pali Canon in Roman script.

The Pali Canon contains three sets of texts: the suttas, which are the discourses the Buddha gave over forty-five years; the Vinaya, which are the texts that describe the monastic discipline in great detail and list the monastic precepts; the Abhidhamma, which are later commentaries that try to analyse, classify and explain the suttas. I did not use any quotations from the Abhidhamma as this collection is a later addition and is extremely complex.

The suttas are divided into five 'Collections' (*Nikaya*): *Middle Length Discourses* (*Majjhima Nikaya*), *Long Discourses* (*Digha Nikaya*), *Connected Discourses* (*Samyutta Nikaya*), *Numerical Discourses* (*Anguttara Nikaya*), *Minor Discourses* (*Khuddaka Nikaya*). In this last collection, one will find a miscellany of shorter texts like the *Dhammapada,* the *Udana,* the *Sutta Nipata,* and the *Therigatha.*

Since 1881 to the present day, scholars have continued to translate and re-translate the Pali Canon into English. As with any translation, it is a work of interpretation and selection of which word in English not only seems accurate but also conveys the idea of the Pali term so that its meaning can be understood by a modern audience. For example, the Pali word *dukkha* is translated generally as 'suffering', but some translators nowadays have started to translate it as 'anguish' or 'stress'. Another example is the word *samma,* which is generally translated as 'right', but some translators have begun to translate it instead as 'whole' or 'authentic'. Recently I was asking a Pali scholar how he would translate a word someone else translates as 'subdue' and he told me that he would have translated it as 'lead away'.

Sacred texts have appeared in a certain context and culture, and been expressed in a specific language. These texts come to us through time and what we read in translation is an approximation, but by studying them and practising their ideas we can make them our own in modern times. However, we need to keep in mind that there can be no pure text and no pure meaning passed on through time, which accords with the main idea of the Buddha that things are impermanent and subject to the flux of conditions.

As I cannot translate from Pali, I could not bring that expertise, but I could choose from my many readings what would be the most appropriate and relevant passages to present from the Pali Canon. Furthermore, being a meditation teacher, I could bring what I saw as most beneficial to a modern public.

In exploring the spirit of the Buddha one could make an extensive presentation of Buddhism and its various developments. But the title for me is a personal title, it is not about Buddhism, it is about the Buddha. The Buddha is the source of Buddhism and in his time he did not know he was creating Buddhism or that his teachings would survive for 2500 years. So in this text I want to go back to the originator and founder of this great religion and cultural movement. Who was he? What did he teach? What were his personal traits? How did he create this new religious current?

It is important to see that the Buddha did not appear out of nowhere with a philosophy already formed, but that he was born in a certain cultural and religious milieu. Often he had to define himself and his teaching in competition with or in opposition to other religious currents. There was a great tradition in his time for religious seekers to test each other and engage in philosophical debates. Moreover, since the teaching of the Buddha is based on conditionality, it seemed important to consider the conditions that gave rise to his search, to his movement and to the practices he taught.

Chapter One explores the life and awakening of the Buddha and shows that from a young age the Buddha seems to have been a thoughtful young man and to have had a high degree of empathy. Moreover, it appears that from the beginning he could see things from different perspectives and that he had often a wide-angle vision. He also seemed to have the ability to take from other traditions ideas which were familiar to his audience and to transform them into something else that fitted more the direction his teaching was taking. In this way people were not being challenged by a new foreign vocabulary but could be brought slowly but steadily to look at religious practices in a very different manner.

The spirit of his teaching can be found in the second chapter but also in the first poem (facing page 1 above) as translated by Andrew Olendzki, a modern Pali scholar. This is a poem resulting from an encounter between the Buddha and Mara, a Buddhist version of the Devil, who often comes in the Buddhist scriptures to taunt and challenge the Buddha. Here Mara is challenging the Buddha to show his 'metaphorical' farming. For the Buddha, one starts with faith, a deep belief in one's capacity to walk the Buddhist path and to awaken. But faith is not enough, so one needs to practise mindfulness and to develop the mind with wisdom and humility.

Ethics is also essential in helping one to use the body optimally without hurting oneself or others, and the Buddha gives special attention to speaking the truth and to communication that helps to develop harmony among people. The Buddha recommends restraint of the senses but not harsh austerities. Again and again I shall point out how he emphasised loving-kindness and compassion.

Another crucial aspect of his teaching is right effort in conjunction with the recognition that intention can be a powerful ally when trying to change. The Buddha does not recommend brute force, but encourages his disciples to engage creatively with inner conditions and outer conditions. His main point is to reflect: what is it that helps one develop wisdom and compassion, and what is it that does not? He is a pragmatist and not an ideologist. In the end, what matters for him is the release from suffering for himself and for everyone else.

In the Buddha's time spiritual teachers were greatly respected, so his disciples would address him as the Blessed One, Lord, Honoured One, and so on. He is not considered a god but as a human being who has attained a great awakening and who can also teach others the path of awakening and the end of suffering. As such he is addressed formally and respectfully. When the Buddhist tradition developed further, the Buddha's status became more and more elevated and the form of address ever more elaborate.

The Buddha mostly referred to himself as the Tathagata, which has often been translated as 'Thus come or Thus gone', but other scholars suggest that it could mean 'The one who is like that' or 'The one who is like he is'. The Buddha generally does not talk about himself in terms of 'I' or 'me' as he is trying to deconstruct a reified sense of self, which can fix one and amplify separation. At the same time it is important to know that Pali does not make great use of personal pronouns as the subject of the sentence is indicated by the ending of the verb. The Buddha in general seems to try to avoid categorical definition and has a multi-perspectival approach.

The third chapter is focused on the community, *sangha* in Pali. The way he created a community and organised it is an essential aspect of the spirit of the Buddha. This allowed his community to be long-lasting and to survive intact for 2500 years while transmitting the Buddha's teaching, discipline and practice up to our present day. This shows that the community structure put in place was remarkably resilient and that the message of the Buddha could be meaningful to different cultures at different times. The Buddha laid a great emphasis on harmony and respect as well as practising and learning together as a means to develop a community which would sustain its members and also hold up to them the ideal of their founder.

One of its interesting characteristics was mutual public confession of one's faults as a means to deal with difficulties and also to use differences as a path of practice.

The fourth chapter is on meditation practices, which form one of the distinctive aspects of the spirit of the Buddha, in that he managed to develop and teach so many different methods of meditation practice that are very effective. Later on, even more methods would be created, but already in the Pali Canon one finds a treasure-house of meditations based on mindfulness and recollection. This seems to indicate that the Buddha was a great religious explorer and an astute observer of the mind and body, and of the means to work with them in a transformative way. In his time seekers already practised concentration, but the Buddha was an innovator in adding penetrative insight to meditation exercises. From then on Buddhist meditation practices would not be reduced to just calming the body and the mind, but would be involved in a deep exploration of one's mental, physical and emotional experiences and their connection with the world.

Chapter Five looks at how compassion is at the root of the Buddha's teachings. In the early Buddhist scriptures one can notice the emphasis laid by the Buddha on loving-kindness, compassion, sympathetic joy and equanimity. The Buddha did not want to disappear into the forest away from the world, even if he found sitting at the root of a tree conducive to meditation. He wanted members of his community to exist with and for the people who supported them. He wanted his monastics to benefit the people around them out of concern and compassion for their well-being and to help relieve their suffering. When Devatta, one of his cousins, suggested that the Buddhist community of monastics become more ascetical and retire from the world, the Buddha refused.

In Chapter Six, dedicated to ethics, one can see that the Buddha thought of ethics as being the basis for spiritual progress. In his time the Buddha moved the focus of the religious quest away from what the world was to how one should behave. He was a great believer in moral agency, which was a departure from the mores of his times. In India 2500 years ago, purity was based on the proper ritual and being born in the higher castes. The Buddha declared and instructed that one's purity and one's ethics were not based on ritual nor on caste, but on one's actions. It was a liberating message, which is being heard to this day in India where millions of untouchables are becoming Buddhists to give themselves freedom and dignity.

The Buddha lived for more than eighty years and during that time travelled to all the different cities and countries around his place of birth in the Ganges plain. He saw different methods of governing and he had to deal with various kings and princes who often were his supporters and came to him for advice on matters of government. Being a great believer in peaceful relations, he often dreamt and hoped for an ideal form of government, which would govern righteously and peacefully without inflicting any harm. This is what I explore in Chapter Seven. This is the one project that he might not have been able to realise during his lifetime but which was partly achieved two hundred years later by King Ashoka once he renounced war and became a Buddhist-inspired monarch.

In the last three chapters I look at what happened after the death of the Buddha. Chapter Eight is focused on transmission. The Buddha did not pass his mantle of authority to anyone, although later Buddhist traditions would create lineages (done backwards) to give themselves authenticity and feel connected to the founder. On his deathbed the Buddha insisted on self-reliance, something he had recommended all his life. He told his followers that they should take his teachings as a refuge. This is why it was so important to keep the teaching accurate and why early on he instituted groups of memorising monastics who could ensure that no errors or different meanings entered the recollection of the discourses of the Buddha.

In *The Spirit of the Buddha* I also wanted to look at the transformation that happened to Buddhism after his founder died. What kind of traditions developed and emerged over the centuries in different countries and different times and cultural contexts? When comparing traditions, one generally looks at the differences, but in Chapter Nine I wanted to look at the similarities not only between traditions but also with the original teachings. In reading Buddhist texts, what strikes me is the connection with the original teachings in the Pali Canon. Although the practices, the cultures, the traditions might look very different, in fact if one looks more closely one finds many similarities and points of convergence like emptiness and not-self, morality and compassion, or the cultivation of quietness and clarity.

In the last chapter I carry on with the theme of continuity and transformation but in relationship to the modern world and look at how twenty-first century Buddhists are adapting Buddhism to a modern, egalitarian, scientific and psychological world. This exploration makes me point out that the Buddha was relevant to his times but also to our modern times as human nature does not seem to have changed very much in terms of the three poisons of greed, hatred and delusion, and in the remedies that one can apply to deal with these powerful negative forces. But the spirit of the Buddha also struck me as revolutionary concerning his notion of equality and his deep knowledge of conditionality, and this might make him actually a man for our time, in which we now find quarks and strings and where we realise that the brain is much more malleable than we previously thought. It seemed to me that with his pragmatic and multi-perspectival approach the Buddha might have been the first deconstructivist and also the first cognitive therapist.

Chapter One

The Life

BEGINNING

I am of Khattiya, Warrior-noble stock. I was reborn into a Khattiya family. I am a Gotama by clan. My life's span is of short length, it is brief and soon over; one who lives long now completes the century or a little more. I became fully enlightened at the foot of an Assatha Banyan tree. My chief disciples are Sariputta and Moggallana. I have had one assembly of disciples, consisting of twelve hundred and fifty monks, all of them arahants. My chief personal attendant now is Bhikkhu Ananda. My father was king Suddhodana, my mother was Queen Maya, and the royal capital was Kapilavatthu.

Digha Nikaya 14 (condensed)

The Buddha rarely talked about himself and his life prior to his awakening. In this passage, condensed by the translator, he presents himself. Gotama is the name of his clan and as a youth he was called Siddhatta Gotama. The legend about the Buddha's life is that he was the prince of a kingdom. This legend was constituted over time and finalised in the *Buddhacarita* written by Ashvagosha in the second century CE. Scholars now believe that the Buddha was born and died in the fifth century BCE, which would make him a contemporary of Socrates. He was born in Lumbini, a small park near the border of Nepal and India, and raised in the nearby town of Kapilavatthu.

Kapilavatthu was the capital of the Sakya republic. This is why the Buddha is also referred to as Sakyamuni, meaning the sage *(muni)* of the Sakya. The Sakya territory seems to have consisted of about ten towns and had a population of roughly 180,000 people, one third living in the towns and the rest in small villages. The Buddha's father, Suddhodana, was the elected head of an aristocratic hereditary ruling class, and as such he had the status and prestige equivalent to the ruler of a small kingdom. Sakya was a vassal state of a much bigger kingdom, Kosala, and the king of Kosala was the overlord of the Sakyans.

The Buddha was a member of a warrior family, though this warrior family also took care of agriculture. As a Khattiya farmer, he was supposed to till the land and to bear arms. The duties of his father were to collect taxes, to make sure public works were undertaken and improved the country, to take care of diplomacy with the overlord and the neighbouring states, and in this to be involved in the regulation of pastures and irrigation rights, and finally to ensure that justice was administered. The overlord himself was in charge of the army and of fighting wars.

The Buddha awakened under a ficus religiosa, which became known as the Bodhi tree. Bodhi means awakening. The ficus religiosa, which is also called a sacred fig, is a type of Banyan fig that grows easily in Nepal and India. One of its other names is Assatha tree. It can become quite large, up to thirty metres tall, and the diameter of its rough trunk can extend to three metres. Its leaves are beautifully heart-shaped with a distinctive long and elegant tip. Because the Buddha attained awakening under such a tree, this tree has become sacred to the Buddhists. Cuttings were taken from the original tree and propagated in other places. One such cutting, which became a large tree, was taken by Sanghamitta, a Buddhist nun, the daughter of King Ashoka (272-231 BCE), to Sri Lanka, where she spread Buddhism. In turn, a cutting of that tree was planted back in India in Bodh Gaya to replace the original tree that had died. Buddhists on pilgrimage revere the descendants of this tree in the town of Bodh Gaya. Trees had an important place in the life of the Buddha and he often recommended meditation at the foot of a tree.

Maya, the chief consort of Suddhodana, was the mother of the Buddha. She died a week after his birth. It was her sister Mahapajapati, another consort of Suddhodana, who raised him. Mahapajapati later became the first Buddhist nun and is revered as such by female Buddhists and especially nuns. Nowadays her name is invoked in many projects associated with women, such as the Mahapajapati Thera College, which is the first Buddhist college for women in Thailand.

Sariputta was the chief disciple of the Buddha, who often praised him for his wisdom and quickness of mind. Moggallana and Sariputta, who both came from Brahmin families, were friends from childhood. They decided to become wandering ascetics together. First they followed a teacher called Sanjaya, who was an agnostic, which means that he did not ascertain anything; to any statement he would say, 'I don't know.' Moggallana and Sariputta, though they respected him, were not fully satisfied with his teaching, so they separated to travel and find the truth. They were supposed to tell each other if they found a great teacher. Sariputta met first a disciple of the Buddha called Assaji. Upon being asked what the teaching of the Buddha was, Assaji said:

Of those things that arise from a cause,
the Buddha has told the cause,
and also what their cessation is:
this is the doctrine of the Great Contemplative.

Upon hearing this, Sariputta achieved some insight and decided to follow the Buddha. He told Mogallana and they both became the Buddha's disciples. Mogallana was renowned for his spiritual powers. After practising with the Buddha, both became arahants, Moggallana a little more quickly, seven days after his ordination, and Sariputta two weeks later. To become an arahant in Buddhism is to become awakened, in an awakening similar to that of the Buddha. The Buddha explained awakening as happening in four stages. In the first stage, there is a loss of belief in self, rites and rituals, and doubt disappears. In the second stage, greed and hatred are weakened. In the third stage, greed and hatred are dissolved. In the fourth stage, which is the arahant stage, conceit, restlessness and ignorance disappear. Moggallana and Sariputta had attained that fourth stage of arahanthood.

A bhikkhu is a man who has received ordination under the Buddha. A woman is called a bhikkhuni. Bhikkhu Ananda, being the son of the brother of the Buddha's father, was the Buddha's first cousin and was the same age as the Buddha. He became a monk two years after the Buddha's awakening. For the first twenty years, the Buddha did not have a regular attendant. After a while, he found this arrangement unsatisfactory as often the attendants refused to obey or they made mistakes. He therefore asked for someone to become his regular attendant and Ananda accepted on the condition that this position would not bring him any benefits. After the Buddha accepted his condition, Ananda attended him for twenty-five years until the Buddha's death. Ananda is important in the Buddhist tradition because he had a very retentive memory and at the first council convened after the Buddha's death he was able to remember and recite all the teachings of the Buddha that he had heard. This is why many suttas start with the words 'Thus I have heard. ... '

> *This thought came to me: 'An uninstructed person, though sure to become old himself and unable to escape ageing feels repelled, humiliated and disgusted when seeing an old and decrepit person, being forgetful of his own situation. Now I too am sure to become old and cannot escape ageing. If, when seeing an old and decrepit person, I were to feel repelled, humiliated or disgusted, that would not be proper for one like myself.' When I reflected thus, monks, all my pride in youthfulness vanished.*
>
> *Again I reflected: 'An uninstructed person, though sure to become ill herself and unable to escape illness, feels repelled, humiliated and disgusted when seeing a sick person, being forgetful of her own situation. Now I too am sure to become ill and cannot escape illness. If, when seeing a sick person, I were to feel repelled, humiliated or disgusted, that would not be proper for one like myself.' When I thus reflected, monks, all my pride in health vanished.*
>
> *Again I reflected: 'An uninstructed person is sure to die himself and cannot escape death; yet when seeing a dead person, he feels repelled, humiliated and disgusted, being forgetful of his own situation. Now I too am sure to die and cannot escape death. If, seeing a dead person, I were to feel repelled, humiliated or disgusted, that would not be proper for one like myself.' When I thus reflected, monks, all my pride in life vanished.*
>
> *Anguttara Nikaya*, III, 38

The Buddha appears to have been a thoughtful young man. Compared with other Sakyans he was in a position of power, riches and privileges, but instead of losing himself in these or abusing them, he seems to have been acutely aware of the equality of humanity in terms of old age, sickness and death. When he reflected in this way, he was a young man in the prime of youth. When one is young it is easy to think of oneself as invincible, full of energy and projects, and to see old age as so far away – a foreign country. The Buddha evidently had a high degree of empathy. He was aware in his bones that youth was transient. He could see people around him getting old and realised that this would happen to him too.

The Buddha's thoughts led him to the same conclusion about illness. Although he seemed to be healthy now, it did not mean that he would always be in good health. Good health was not assured, even if he came from a wealthier family. He realised that he was not immune to illness. Here we can recognise some particularities of the spirit of the Buddha – reflection, empathy, equality – which must have made him somewhat different from other young men of his age and of his caste. He did not feel superior and exempt from the exigencies of life, in spite of his higher status. In that way he did not feel proud of his health; on the contrary, he was aware of its unreliability.

When one is alive and well it is easy to think and furthermore to feel that one is immortal or eternal. From our point of view, it is other people who die. As long as we are alive, it has not happened to us. It is interesting that for the Buddha there was an intense awareness of life and death, of the idea that one could not exist without the other. He could not see something without also seeing its opposite, seeing its other possibilities. This is another feature of the character of the Buddha that we are going to find later in his teaching: his ability to look at different angles, not to be limited to only one viewpoint, but to consider different perspectives. Even at a young age, he appears to have had wide-angle vision. Already he seemed not to be limited by his caste, his status, his ordinary enjoyments and expectations. He saw further than what might be expected of a young man in his position.

Before my enlightenment, while I was still only an unenlightened Bodhisattva, being myself subject to birth, ageing, ailment, death, sorrow and defilement, I sought after what was also subject to these things. Then I thought: Why, being myself subject to birth, ageing ailment, death, sorrow and defilement, do I seek after what is also subject to these things? Suppose, being myself subject to these things, having understood the danger in them, I seek after the unborn, unageing unailing deathless, sorrowless and undefiled supreme security from bondage, nibbana.

Majjhima Nikaya, 26

Here we can see the Buddha at a turning-point in his life. Up to that moment he went along with what was common to all. He tried to fulfil the duties of his caste, to enjoy being young, participate in the ordinary things in life – creating wealth, having a spouse, trying to procreate, playing with friends, indulging his senses, being covetous, angry and foolish. But then he reflected – is that all there is to life? He started to hope that there might be another way. He wondered if he could seek after something else, something that was other, apart, away from ageing, sickness and death. That something would help him not to be covetous, angry or foolish. That something or that way would lead to liberation.

Nibbana (Nirvana) means blowing out, as a fire blows out because of a lack of fuel. In a Buddhist context it means blowing out the three fires of greed, hatred and delusion. The Buddha had the skilful tendency to take concepts belonging to other traditions that would be familiar to his audience and to transform them into something else. In India at that time the Brahmins had to tend and keep lit three sacrificial fires in their home every day, so the Buddha took this idea of the three fires and gave it a more practical and personally transformational purpose. Now the task of the Buddha's disciples was to extinguish the fires that kept burning within them. Later on, the metaphor of the three fires was lost and replaced by the idea of the three poisons of greed, hatred and delusion.

In the *Maggasamyutta Sutta* (7) the Buddha says that nibbana and the deathless are the freedom from greed, hatred and delusion. In a sacred text of Brahminism, the Katha Upanishad, the primal is seen as unborn, eternal and everlasting, and it also says that if one is killed, one is not actually killed, though the body is. Again the Buddha takes a Brahmin concept, which is metaphysical, and turns it into a practical possibility. For the Buddha, the idea of the unborn or the deathless is not that one is never born again or never dies literally, but that in this life there is the possibility to dissolve greed, hatred and delusion. If one does not commit acts out of greed, hatred and delusion, then one will not commit defilements and one will be free from the bondage in which clinging keeps one.

The Buddha does not see nibbana as a special, metaphysical place to go to but as a process of dissolution that one can achieve here and now. It is important to point out, however, that over centuries and with the development of different Buddhist traditions nibbana took on a more rarefied and metaphysical meaning. At the same time, it is interesting to consider the recent teachings of Venerable Buddhadasa, a great Thai monk (1906-93) who tried to go back to that original meaning of nibbana and even beyond. He said: '. . . I try to point out that the social good and acting for the benefit of society are prerequisites of travelling beyond to nibbana.'

Before the Buddha was awakened he called himself a bodhisattva – a bodhisattva simply being someone who aspires to awakening (bodhi). Over time the idea about what it meant to be a bodhisattva for the Buddha was developed and it started to acquire great complexity. In order to become a Buddha, the bodhisattva first has to make the great resolution to become awakened, and for this resolution to be effective, the bodhisattva requires eight conditions. He must be reborn as a human being; he must be born in a male body; he has to be a recluse at the time of his resolution; he must declare his intention before a Buddha; he should be able to have states of deep concentration; he must be prepared to sacrifice everything and his aspiration must be resolute and unshakable. This list seems to be an analysis of the circumstances and conditions of Siddhatta Gotama used retrospectively. For our modern sensibilities, it is hard to see how awakening would have to be gender specific, since greed, hatred and delusion and the liberation from them do not appear to be gender specific.

Then another list appears giving the five great sacrifices the bodhisattva is to make in order to be able to become a Buddha. These are renouncing his wife, his children, his kingdom, his limbs and his life. Again for modern times, especially for women and mothers, this is a little difficult to understand. We are told different things about the Buddha, and why and how he left his wife and child. It is generally thought that the Buddha left to make his quest for awakening when he was twenty-nine years old, just after his son was born. This would mean that marrying when he was around sixteen, the age at which people were betrothed in those days, he would have lived with only one wife, who remained childless for thirteen years. It seems to make more sense that he married at sixteen and that as soon as a son was born to take over his inheritance he was able to leave, especially as his father was healthy and continued to live on for many years. Why did he leave his son and wife behind? It looks as though his awareness of impermanence and suffering was so strong that he felt compelled to do something about it in a radical way. Furthermore, in that society and with his family status, he knew that his wife and child would be well taken care of.

THE SEARCH

Later, while still young, a black-haired boy endowed with the blessing of youth, in the prime of life I shaved off my hair and beard – though my mother and father wished otherwise and wept with tearful faces – and I put on the yellow robe and went forth from the home life into homelessness.

Majjhima Nikaya, 26

In the legend, the Buddha is seen leaving stealthily in the dead of night, but here in these words he tells us that he informed his parents of his decision. His parents were upset because they had great hopes for him. Here we have two important concepts for the Buddha: the ideas of home life and of homelessness. He reiterated several times that he felt that the home life was crowded and full of dust, while the homeless life seemed wide open. As the elder son of a prosperous farming family, it is unlikely that he himself would have worked in the field, but he would have been aware of how important it was to have a good harvest and to give a part of it as tribute to the king of Kosala. He did not find it easy to be a householder and live a perfect life, as he said, *'pure as a polished shell'*. For him, a householder life was full of duties and constraints, which made it difficult to cultivate a life free from defilements.

The Buddha was born at a key moment in Indian history. In his epoch it became possible for people to leave their home life and to be fed by the rest of the population. Farmers began to create an economic surplus when tilling the land of the rich plains surrounding the riverbanks of the Ganges. This economic surplus enabled the first great cities to be built and monarchies to develop. One of the economic consequences for the population was that armies could be raised and fed, and wandering mendicants could leave a productive life and become dependent on alms.

A specialist on the history of India in the sixth and seventh centuries BCE suggests that various spiritual movements arose that had new spiritual goals. These movements consisted of people who were critical of the Vedic-Brahmin sacrificial systems and who wanted to find new religious ways. Professor H.W. Schumann categorised them in four main ways. One group was formed of people who followed the Upanishads and were an unorthodox offshoot of the Vedic tradition. Another group consisted of materialists; they are often mentioned in the suttas as engaging in debates with the Buddha. The third group was formed by ascetics of various types who did meditation exercises and practised self-mortification such as fasting or maintaining one posture for a long period of time. The last group is of wandering mendicants. Professor Schumann defines them as experimenters in religion: some were sophists, some were fatalists, and they had many different ideas.

Shaving the hair and beard was a sign of renunciation of home life, of leaving behind the vanities of the body. To show complete renunciation, Siddhatta Gotama also renounced his fine clothes and wore simple clothes of one colour, in this case yellow. At that time wanderers made their clothes out of scraps of material found lying around. They used to cut the usable pieces, sewed them together and dyed them using various natural dyes. They generally were of an earth colour – ochre and yellow in this region of India. The colour was intended to be different from the more flamboyant and diverse colours used by ordinary people. The colour might also have been chosen for its quality of not showing the dirt too much.

To this day monks and nuns shave their hair and it is their first sign of renunciation upon entering the monastery. As to the clothes, over time monastics from different countries developed different styles in various colours, according to the dyes available in their country as well as the climate and the culture. Some monastic robes are still bright yellow, some saffron, some orange, some brown, some maroon. In China, Korea, Vietnam or Japan, the clothes can be darker in colour, such as black or grey, or lighter like pale blue, but the ceremonial robes tend to keep a taint of brown, yellow or gold by association with the colour worn by the Buddha.

I thought: This Dhamma does not lead to dispassion, to jading of lust,
to cessation, to peace, to direct knowledge, to enlightenment, to nibbana,
but only to the Base Consisting of Nothingness. I was not satisfied with
that Dhamma. I left it to pursue my search.

Majjhima Nikaya, 26

Siddhatta Gotama joined the life of wandering mendicants, those who were looking for a new way of liberation. First he joined the group of Alara

Kalama, a teacher who claimed to have attained the direct knowledge of nothingness. Siddhatta Gotama practised under his direction and attained the direct knowledge of nothingness, but he found that this did not lead to what he was searching for – dispassion, awakening and nibbana. Although Alara Kalama invited Siddhatta to teach together with him, Siddhatta declined and looked for another teacher.

Then Siddhatta went to Uddaka Ramaputta, who was known for having learnt from his father what led to the 'sphere of neither perception nor non-perception". Again, Siddhatta Gotama had a direct experience of this 'sphere of neither perception nor non-perception", whereas Uddaka Ramaputta had merely heard about it from his father. This time Uddaka Ramaputta proposed to him the sole leadership of his school. However, Siddhatta Gotama had again found that this was not what he was looking for. He therefore desisted and went on searching further for what would really lead him to awakening and nibbana.

We do not know exactly what kind of methods these two teachers taught Siddhatta Gotama. Afterwards the Buddha only mentioned what the specific attainment was. It is thought that during this time the Buddha learnt meditation techniques that used concentration and led to absorption states. It seems that the Buddha had the remarkable ability of mastering these techniques and of experiencing their goal relatively easily. Throughout his life the Buddha would make use of these concentration techniques when it seemed appropriate. If one concentrates on a particular object in meditation in a certain way, it is possible to experience states where one is extremely calm and at peace, and where one experiences the world and consciousness in a different way.

> *Again there are some recluses and Brahmins who assert and believe that purification comes through food, and they say: 'Let us live on beans"* *... 'Let us live on sesame" ... 'Let us live on rice' ... Now I have had experience of eating a single bean ... a single sesame seed ... a single rice grain a day ... Yet, Sariputta, by such conduct, by such practice, by such performance of austerities, I did not attain any superhuman states, any distinction in knowledge and vision worthy of the noble ones. Why not? Because I did not attain that noble wisdom, which, when attained, is noble and emancipating, and leads the one who practises it to the complete dissolution of suffering....*
>
> *Majjhima Nikaya, 12*

It is thought that from six months to about a year the Buddha was with these two teachers, but since their methods did not work for him, he decided to try the way of the ascetics. For a few years he therefore endured endless austerities, of the types that were popular at his time. And because he had great determination and endurance, he achieved all these difficult feats – of eating a single rice grain a day, for example, for days on end. Again, however, although he could reach a certain goal with these methods – the mastery of his body, feelings and mind, thereby experiencing some knowledge and vision – this did not resolve the problem of suffering and of the three fires.

The Buddha therefore finally decided to do something totally different and on his own. At some point during his years of austerities, five other ascetics who had been impressed by his great strength of purpose and achievements had gathered around him. When, however, he decided to give up the way of the ascetics, they were dismayed and distanced themselves from him. So now he was truly alone and could only rely and depend on himself. These are two characteristics of the spirit of the Buddha: on the one hand, he was able to question; to try different things; and on the other hand, he was able to go on his own, to depend just upon himself, and later he would encourage others to do the same.

At that point he remembered an episode from his childhood. While his father was working in the fields, he sat quietly under a rose apple tree and entered a state of deep calm and peace. He found that this state was accompanied by thinking and exploring. There was also pleasure, but a pleasure that had 'nothing to do with sensual pleasures or unwholesome things'. It seemed to be a state close to what he was looking for – to be freed from the three fires of greed, hatred and delusion. He wondered if this was not the way forward, to develop this state and to see where it would lead him. So he took the food offered to him by a young woman and went and sat at the foot of an Assatha banyan tree. He decided that he would not leave this place until he had fulfilled his search.

AWAKENING

It is owing to the development
of virtue, concentration, and understanding,
that I have reached enlightenment.

Samyutta Nikaya, IV, 1

The Buddha sat beneath the Bodhi tree for seven days and on the seventh day, upon seeing dawn, he reached awakening. It was based, as he said, on the cultivation of virtue, concentration and understanding. Here we find the three trainings that the Buddha taught all his life – morality, meditation and wisdom. Virtue or living an ethical life was an important basis for his awakening, and again and again he encourages monks, nuns and lay people to lead a moral life. An ethical life for him meant a life that does not cause suffering to oneself or to others. It is a life where one brings great attention to one's actions and their effects. It is a code of ethics based not so much on rules and regulations, but on intention, activities and results.

The concentration, he has learned previously, is seen by the Buddha as an important element of the meditation. One needs to be able to concentrate on an object in one's experience for some time in order to be able to have a more stable and peaceful mind. Over time, with concentration one is less identified with one's thoughts, feelings or sensations. One is also less caught up in them and so less distracted by them. In this way one no longer follows all one's tendencies and negative habits, which might lead one to commit unskilful actions. Here one can see that ethics and concentration are linked. In turn, if one is behaving unethically it will be hard to concentrate in a meditative way.

Understanding is also part of the key: the Buddha had not only experienced a special state of meditation but had also understood something that he had not previously seen and known. Up to that point his understanding was limited to the concepts of his times, which were influenced deeply by the Vedic culture that dictated certain rituals and certain sacrifices as the basis and the end of the spiritual life. His understanding went further than that. He looked at human beings, their actions and their relationships with the world in the here and now, and saw conditionality as one of the fundamental principles one could experience and understand in order to attain awakening.

At the end of the seven days, he emerged from that concentration, and in the first watch of the night his mind was occupied with dependent arising in forward order thus: That comes to he when there is this; that arises with the arising of this.

Udana, I, 1-3

Here the Buddha becomes aware of the law of causality, that everything has a cause, that a cause has an effect, that everything that arises will pass away. This conditionality is seen as applying to everything and thus becomes a universal principle. The Buddha explains that existence depends on different conditioning factors. This is a pluralist notion, in opposition to the notion of the Upanishads, which is based on the unifying concept of an immortal soul and non-differentiation. According to the Upanishad vision, everything is essentially one and identical with the absolute, and differences are just delusory and unreal. The Buddha did not assert that there is an immortal soul or an absolute behind all things. He did not see any special essence, but he saw things as coming about conditionally and life as a continuous process of becoming.

This led the Buddha to reject rites and rituals as prerequisites for the continuance of the world or the attainment of salvation. At that time chosen people would perform certain rites so that the gods would perform particular actions that would benefit the world and its people. The Buddha bypassed that system and saw that each person can determine his or her own life according to the conditions that form them and also according to how they relate to those conditions. He therefore encouraged people to discover conditions. For him, awakening was not beyond conditions, on the contrary it made one discover and explore conditions so that one saw clearly what led to greed, hatred and delusion, and what led to non-greed, non-hatred, and non-delusion. He was interested in what was going to help a person dissolve the conditions that created suffering in the first place.

After his awakening, the Buddha went back to Sarnath where the five ascetics who had left him were, and they became his first disciples. Following this, he converted people whenever he met them and they heard his teaching. One of his important converts was King Bimbisara of Magadha, whose capital was Rajagaha. This town was quite extensive and was a well-known place for brahmins and various other spiritual groups who often engaged each other in debates, as was the tradition among these religious seekers. This town was second in importance only to Savatthi, the capital of Kosala. King Bimbisara was five years younger than the Buddha and had been a king for sixteen years when they met. When he heard the Buddha's discourse, he was struck by its wisdom and decided to become a lay follower of the Buddha, although this did not mean that he stopped giving alms to others. Upon the king's conversion, many other Magadhans started to follow the Buddha as well. After staying a little while in Rajagaha, the Buddha went back to his home of Sakya.

It would have taken the Buddha about sixty days to reach Kapilavatthu. After an absence of eight years, his homecoming was somewhat tense, but it was upon this occasion that Rahula, his son, entered the order together with Nanda, his half-brother, as well as Ananda and Devadatta, both cousins. The Buddha then wandered between different places in the north of India. He often went to Rajagaha, where he liked to meditate on Vulture Peak and lived in the Bamboo Grove, so that these are important places for Buddhist pilgrims. He also spent time in Savatthi, capital of Kosala, where King Pasenadi too became a follower, and made visits to Vesali, the capital of the Licchavis. From time to time the Buddha also visited Sakya and on his second visit he helped to resolve a conflict about access to the waters of the Rohini river.

TEACHING

Two thoughts often occur to a Buddha, accomplished and fully enlightened: The thought of harmlessness and the thought of seclusion. A Buddha takes pleasure and delights in non-affliction, and with that it often occurs to him: 'By such behaviour I afflict none, timid or bold'. A Buddha takes pleasure and delight in seclusion, and with that it often occurs to him: 'What is unprofitable has been abandoned'.

Itivuttaka, II, ii, 1

Throughout his life the Buddha put a great emphasis on harmlessness. For him an essential component of the path is non-harming, every way possible he wanted to avoid causing suffering. This non-harming, however, is not forced or dour but on the contrary it gave him pleasure and delight. This is something that he learnt from his ascetic practices and his renunciation of them. To alleviate suffering one does not have to cause more suffering. One easy way to experience joy is to be harmless. And again, he pointed out that it is a harmlessness directed to all, not just to one category of people. Whether the person is timid or bold, he does not want to harm anyone. It seems that he means that he does not want to take advantage of the timidity of one person and take the opportunity to cause harm. At the same time, he is not going to want to take revenge or to reply in kind if someone is arrogant or aggressive.

Again and again we find the Buddha trying to alleviate conflicts, whether among his own people, other people, or his community of monks and nuns. In everything he did he tried to cultivate harmlessness and encourage others to do the same. He was a great advocate of peace and at the same time he was aware that he himself could not change certain conditions beyond his control. He could control himself and he could endeavour to lead a blameless life. He could encourage others to do likewise, but he could not force conditions or people. This is why at the end of his life he tried but failed to prevent a great tragedy, the massacre of the Sakyans by Vidudhaba, the son of King Pasenadi. Three times he intervened and asked the army of Vidudhaba to spare the Sakyans and to stop its advance, but they refused to listen to him and the Sakyans were annihilated.

Another characteristic of the Buddha is his love of seclusion and of meditating in the forest. For us it might appear like a sad thing to do, to meditate by oneself, away from everybody, but for the Buddha it a great solace. Again and again he will express his joy in meditating in solitude. He will take the time to leave his community and dwell by himself. The fact that he has attained awakening does not mean that he stops meditation; on the contrary, throughout his life he will continue to practise meditation assiduously and thereby encourage his followers to do the same. This love of seclusion is also a special aspect of the homeless life. In seclusion, in meditation, one abandons all entanglements with what is unprofitable, which for the Buddha would be entanglement with greed, hatred and delusion. The homeless life has few needs and requirements and the secluded life even fewer.

THE END

Conditions are subject to decay. Tread the path with care.
Digha Nikaya, 16, 6, 7

For about forty-five years, the Buddha travelled and taught around the Ganges basin in what are now the Indian states of Bihar and Uttar Pradesh. For three months every year he and his community would retire for what were called the *vassa*, also known as the rains, to meditate and teach in one place. Owing to the heaviness of the rains during the monsoon, it had been decided it would be better for the monastics and the surrounding environment not to travel, so as not to trample any life forms under foot. Over time, people had offered to the Buddha places to gather; gardens and shelters were given to him and his community by the nobility or merchants. Nowadays some of these important places such as Vesali and Savatthi are on the pilgrimage route. One can generally find a tank of water surrounded by trees and bamboos and the remains of cells where the monks and the nuns meditated in centuries past.

The Buddha was generally on good terms with the kings of his time, who often came to pay their respects or to ask for his advice. They were of the same generation. Over time, however, there arose a younger generation of more ambitious and aggressive individuals. Bimbisara's son, Ajatasattu, had his father starved to death and Pasenadi's position was usurped by his son, Vidudhaba. At the same time the last few republics were taken over by bigger monarchies.

Devadatta, one of the ordained cousins of the Buddha, also had ambition and wanted to take over the sangha from the Buddha. The Buddha, who thought him too arrogant and unwise, did not want him to lead the sangha. Devadatta therefore broke away and took some monks with him, but Sariputta and Mogallana skilfully brought them back. Later, six months before the Buddha died, Mogallana was assassinated by bandits and Sariputta died two weeks later.

Devadatta had associated himself with Ajatasattu and together they tried to kill the Buddha, but they did not succeed. On one occasion a boulder nearly hit him and his foot was injured by a shard. The final part of the Buddha's life could therefore be considered tragic, even if he had succeeded in his ministry. The Buddha was by then about eighty and knew his end was coming. His foot was painful and his digestion impaired, so that he became quite weak. A meal of 'pigs delight' (interpreted as mushrooms by some and as innards of pig by others) caused his last illness and his death.

The quotation above was uttered by the Buddha just before he died. When his followers were lamenting his forthcoming death, he told them clearly that 'conditions are subject to decay'. He was an awakened being but he was also a conditioned being, and so as all conditioned beings arise and pass away, he too was passing away. His death is called the paranibbana, in which he is seen as entering final nibbana, final peace. He did not entrust the sangha to anyone, again a sign that he wanted his disciples to be self-reliant and independent. He enjoined his followers 'to tread the path with care'. Moreover, he told them that the only teacher they needed, the only thing they could rely on, was the dhamma, i.e. his teachings.

Chapter 2

The Dhamma, The Teachings

THE FOUR NOBLE TRUTHS

Bhikkhus, there are these Four Noble Truths: the Noble Truth of Suffering, the Noble Truth of the Origin of Suffering, the Noble Truth of the Cessation of Suffering, and the Noble Truth of the Way Leading to the Cessation of Suffering. A Buddha, accomplished and fully enlightened, is so called because of his discovery of these four Noble Truths.

Samyutta Nikaya, LVI, 23

The word dhamma (in Pali; dharma in Sanskrit) was already found in the brahmanical tradition, where it meant the law of the universe and also the duty of each person. The Buddha used this term to refer to his teachings, but also sometimes to the way things work, or simply to denote things or phenomena in general. The Buddha taught for forty-five years and he was aware that for his teachings to spread and to survive accurately, they needed to be memorised and recited by a group, so groups of monks were set up to recite and memorise certain discourses. They would meet regularly to recite together specific teachings of the Buddha. The body of teachings was transmitted orally in this way until they were written down three hundred years later on palm leaves in Sri Lanka.

In his first teaching, called 'Turning the Wheel of Dhamma', which was addressed to the five ascetics in the Deer Park in Sarnath, the Buddha sets out the four noble truths. In these four truths he indicates what concerns him and what he has awakened to. Again, the fact that the noble truths are divided into four shows the characteristic of the Buddha to look carefully at processes and analyse them. His truths are not truths that one needs to believe in because they are metaphysical and pointing to something beyond anything one can imagine. On the contrary, his truths are about life and the experience of life as one lives it day to day.

The Buddha's concern is suffering. He is not saying that everything is suffering, but that suffering exists. For him, suffering is being subject to sickness, ageing and death. Moreover, it is failing to have what one wants, losing what one likes, getting what one does not like, and not losing what one does not like. It is also being separated from the people or the things that one loves. For the Buddha, therefore, suffering is the practical and actual suffering of what I feel when I am ill or when I lose my house.

The Buddha's noble truths are not about how the universe works and what is the fate and meaning of humanity in the universe, but more an understanding of the underpinnings of what brings suffering and how to undo it. The second noble truth is therefore about the origin of the suffering, which for the Buddha is craving, that is, in general, wanting what is pleasant and rejecting what is unpleasant. In other words, craving comes from the three fires – greed, hatred and delusion. The Buddha is not saying that we do not have needs but that we have to look carefully at our likes and dislikes and how these cause us suffering.

The third noble truth is the cessation of suffering. The Buddha is saying that there is a way out of suffering and that he has understood and experienced it. The cessation of suffering will only happen with the fading away, the letting go, the abandoning of craving. The Buddha is suggesting that there is a way to be free and independent from craving, that anyone can experience this for herself or himself. Anyone can attain it as the Buddha has attained it.

The last truth is the way leading to the cessation of suffering. The Buddha is like a doctor who first makes a diagnosis: there is suffering. Then he examines the causes of the suffering and makes a prognosis of recovery from the suffering. And finally he gives a course of treatment, which is what he calls the 'path with eight branches'. Here the Buddha presents us with a multiple method to deal with the complexity of experiences and the world.

Of these Four Noble truths, the Noble Truth of Suffering must be penetrated by the full knowledge of suffering, the Noble truth of the Origin of Suffering must be penetrated by abandoning craving, the Noble Truth of the cessation of Suffering must be penetrated by realising the cessation of craving, the Noble Truth of the Way Leading to the Cessation of Suffering must be penetrated by maintaining in being the Noble Eightfold Path.

Samyutta Nikaya, LVI, 27

As mentioned above, these four noble truths are not statements of faith but they are things to carry out. Like a course of treatment, it is something that we must apply. The first truth urges us to know suffering fully. The Buddha seems to be aware of a tendency in human beings to try to avoid suffering by not appearing to see it, by going away from it, by masking it. The Buddha is saying that it would be more advisable to know suffering for what it is. He is not saying that we should create more suffering in order really to know it, but when suffering appears, how does it feel – in the body, the mind, the heart, in the conditions we find ourselves in? When we suffer, how do we experience it in the moment? Not in the past, not in the future, but right here and now, can we fully know suffering?

The second truth asks us to abandon craving; basically it asks us to abandon the three fires of greed, hatred and delusion. To want something, to be desperate enough for it to do anything to get it regardless of the suffering we might cause ourselves and others in the process, this is a strong force. The Buddha is stating that it is possible to abandon it as he has abandoned it. Can we imagine how it would feel not to have hate in our heart? What would it require for us to let it go?

The third truth is the realisation of the cessation of craving. The Buddha is saying that this is possible, that all human beings have the possibility to realise what he has realised. As such, the four noble truths are things to do but also things to aspire to. They are truths because they are not like myths imagined and dreamed about, but they can be actual experiences. In the same way that one can experience and know suffering, one can know and experience liberation from craving. This is why these truths are noble. Suffering itself is not noble but the realisation of the truth about it is ennobling.

In the fourth truth we are asked to maintain in being the noble eightfold path. We have to cultivate this path continuously, so we start by knowing suffering, then we see craving, let go of it, and cultivate the path. It is by knowing suffering fully that we shall be able to see clearly the cause of suffering. Seeing directly the cause of suffering will lead us to let go of it. Who wants to continue to suffer? In this way we shall start to experience briefly the cessation of craving and that will enable us to start on the path and to cultivate it. In turn, cultivating the path will help us to know suffering better, to see craving more clearly, to let go of it more often, which in turn will make us practise the path even more.

THE EIGHTFOLD PATH

And what, monks, is the Noble Truth of the Way of practice leading to the Cessation of Suffering? It is just this Noble Eightfold Path, namely: Right View, Right Thought, Right Speech, Right Action, Right Livelihood, Right Effort, Right Mindfulness, and Right Concentration.

Digha Nikaya, 22

In the eightfold path we find the three Buddhist trainings that led the Buddha to his awakening: wisdom – right view and right thought; ethics – right speech, right action, right livelihood; and meditation – right effort, right mindfulness, right concentration. 'Right' is the translation of the Pali word *samma*, which can also mean correct, just, total, whole, real. It could be interpreted also as authentic. It is not so much that there is a right view that is right for all times as opposed to a wrong view. It is rather the idea of a view that is more authentic and corresponds more with the way things work, with the way things happen to be – the notion that things arise upon conditions and pass away. Right action is not a fixed right action, it is an action that is conditioned by love and respect. It is an action that considers the consequences of our actions in terms of whether or not they cause suffering. Right mindfulness enables us to practise in such a way that we become more aware of suffering and of craving. The word right is therefore not used in a totalising way but refers to something that is more skilful and appropriate in terms of knowing suffering and letting go of craving.

The path for the Buddha is multiple and involves all aspects of our lives. First it has to do with how we view the world and what kind of thoughts we are having. Then it considers how we speak, how we communicate with others, how we act and how we live, how we earn our living and sustain our life. Finally it looks at how we use our energy, how we can be aware and how we can focus. So we start by looking internally, then externally, and then internally again. The Buddha is concerned with the interaction between our inner world and the outer world.

THE MIDDLE WAY

There are these two extremes that ought not to be cultivated by one who has gone forth. What two? There is devotion to pursuit of pleasure in sensual desires, which is low, coarse, vulgar, ignoble and harmful; and there is devotion to self-mortification, which is painful, ignoble and harmful. The middle way discovered by a Buddha avoids both these extremes; it gives vision and understanding, and leads to peace, to direct knowledge, to enlightenment, to nibbana. And what is the middle way? It is the Noble Eightfold Path.

Samyutta Nikaya, LVI, 11

The Buddha equates the noble eightfold path with the middle way. This is an essential notion for the Buddha, the idea of cultivating the middle way. We do not try too hard and at the same time we do not try too little. The Buddha learnt this from his own life. When he just indulged in sensual pleasures in his youth, he did not find this satisfying. It seems that the experience that finally pushed him to give up was when, after a day of pleasure with dancing girls, that night he saw them sleeping and looking dishevelled. At that moment he experienced the emptiness and the futility of basing one's life solely on the pursuit of sensual pleasures, which seemed to him so transient and evanescent. But the Buddha also experienced severe austerities for many years, when he became extremely thin, but he did not find this satisfying as it did not bring him peace and contentment. The Buddha therefore wanted to steer a path avoiding these two extremes.

The Buddha considers these two extremes problematic because they are harmful. Pleasures of the senses are harmful in the sense that if we get lost in them, we will not aspire to awakening, to liberation from suffering and craving. They are also painful because they cannot last for ever. So we feel elated and depressed, experiencing pleasure and then feeling let down as it disappears, rather as an addict enjoys the high, feels the low so much more, and thus needs to get high again.

Austerities and asceticism are not the solution either as they make us disregard the body and inflict pain on it. We might learn endurance, but this will not lead to a quiet and peaceful mind as we are constantly fighting the body. To be aware of the body and to use it skilfully and kindly was part of the Buddha's teachings. Again, the Buddha is leading more towards inclusiveness than exclusiveness. He is not presenting perfection but the middle way, though over the centuries following his death, perfection and idealism were to return.

RIGHT VIEW

When one understands how form, feeling, perception, formations and consciousness (and how the eye sees, and so on) are impermanent, one thereby possesses right view.

Samyutta Nikaya, XXII, 51

The Buddha thinks that the way we look at the world, the way we understand it, will have an impact on the way we are and behave, so the eightfold path starts by right view. This quotation presents two important ideas of the Buddha. The first one is how he analyses, defines and explains the person in terms of the 'five aggregates', the five constituents of the person: form, feeling, perception, formations, consciousness. Form represents matter; it refers to our body and the way it experiences the world through the senses. The Buddha sees the body not as restricted by itself but in its interaction with the world and the conditions surrounding it. Feeling refers to the subjective tone of our experience, the tonality of pleasant, unpleasant and neither-pleasant-nor-unpleasant; this tonality is immediately present in any momentary experience we have. Perception is how we make sense of the world, how we respond to the world. Formation is one translation of the Pali word *sankhara*. It is a difficult word to translate. It means that which puts things together through actions, that part of us that acts. It can also be translated as mental formations or volition. Consciousness is the way we are aware of all these things in a unified manner.

So the Buddha says that right view is to know that these five constituents of the person are impermanent. Right view is therefore to know for ourselves that the body and what the body senses are impermanent, that feelings are impermanent, that perceptions are impermanent, that formations are impermanent, and that consciousness is impermanent. In a way, it is to understand deeply that everything that we experience in and outside of ourselves is impermanent.

Apart from impermanence, another aspect of right view is causality and conditionality. It is to know and experience that things come from a cause; that things are caused by other things; that they do not exist independently of the things that have formed them. But also it is to know that as conditions arise they will pass away, which takes us back to impermanence. Moreover, it is causality in terms of the ripening of action. There is a cause and there is a result. If we are dreaming and not taking care when we walk down a steep staircase, we are more likely to fall. If someone causes us suffering by robbing us, we understand that stealing causes pain and we will not do it ourselves. One important aspect of right view is to be clear about the four noble truths, not to believe in them as sacred truths, but to understand them in such a way that one starts to act upon them.

RIGHT THOUGHT

And what, monks, is Right Thought? It is the thought of renunciation, the thought of non-ill-will, the thought of harmlessness. This, monks, is called Right Thought.

Digha Nikaya, 22

Right thought is often translated as right intention in order to make clear the difference between right view and right thought. Right view is about our cognitive faculty. Right thought or intention uses our ability to have a purpose, to have the intention to transform ourselves. So the thoughts that inspire us in right thought are thoughts of renunciation, of non-hatred and harmlessness. There are two types of renunciation. We can renounce out of restraint, by intentionally not doing something that we would like to do, or we can renounce something because we see no point in doing it any more.

The first renunciation involves becoming conscious of the consequences of one's desires. This is an important part of the message of the Buddha, to question our desires, from wanting another piece of chocolate cake that is not going to help our digestion or our waistline, to wanting some material things that we cannot afford or that we already have in a different model, to feeling attracted to someone who is not attracted to us. What is the difference between a need and a desire? The Buddha thought that we need to breathe, to drink, to eat, to wear clothes, to have a shelter, and to have medicine when we are ill. We could also say that we need to learn, to work and to have some companionship. What would be the middle way in terms of these needs? What is the least we could need? What is the most we could want? How does it feel when we satisfy a need and move on? What is the thirst that is left when our desires feel barely satisfied? Our desires can keep us fairly busy and frustrated. The intention of renunciation would help us to see simplicity as something to aspire to, so leading to peace and contentment.

The second type of renunciation refers to the stage where one does not have the desire to do something that one used to do. One does not feel the need for it any more, it has lost its appeal. Moreover, when he was practising in the forest, the Buddha recognised that thoughts driven by desire did not bring him peace, whereas the thought of renunciation did.

Right thought or intention is also an aspiration to good will. The basic axiom of the Buddha is that suffering is painful for us and for others. When we dislike or hate something or someone, we are obsessed negatively by that thing or that person, and that thing or that person is on our mind constantly. This causes us a great deal of stress and suffering and generally does not help us to deal creatively with the difficulty. Moreover, hateful thoughts will lead us to say hateful words or commit hateful actions, a process that again generally does not solve the problem and might lead to more suffering. Prior to his awakening, the Buddha noticed that when he had good will in his mind, it helped him to feel better, to be more at peace, to talk and act more peacefully.

Right thought or intention is also an aspiration to harmlessness. Suffering being the Buddha's main concern, his credo is not to harm. This is his main objective, not to cause any harm to any living things. The Buddha does not see this as an end in itself but as a practice that will lead to awakening. It is back to conditionality and causality. If one does not entertain harmful thoughts or intentions, one is much less likely to cause harm intentionally and more likely to experience a peaceful state of mind. The Buddha saw that intention is a powerful thing. If we intend something, we are considering the possibility of something in our mind, and this consideration and reflection makes it more present and actual for us, so that we are more likely to act in that way.

RIGHT SPEECH

And what, monks, is Right Speech? Refraining from lying, refraining from slander, refraining from harsh speech, refraining from frivolous speech. This is called Right Speech.

Digha Nikaya, 22

The Buddha encourages his disciples to become more aware of how they speak and what they say. He shed light on four different types of speech that he considered either harmful or unhelpful. It seems that the Buddha was quite observant and noticed ways he might have spoken in his youth, or ways people address each other that seemed to him to cause suffering or to be unskilful. He discourages untruth. He does not mean that we have to say everything that passes through our mind that seems true, but that when we speak we should try to be truthful and not to tell lies intentionally so as to mislead people or take advantage of them. It is not the lie in itself that is problematic but the consequences of the lie and the intention behind it.

The Buddha also makes us look at how we might either disparage others in order to increase our own importance or slander others to depreciate them in the eyes of other people. The Buddha invites us first to look and see if we say anything that could be called slandering, then how we do it and why we do it. When he draws attention to harsh speech it also makes us consider the tone of our speech. The words themselves might be proper, but maybe the tone in which we say them could be aggressive or dismissive and so the tone more than the words themselves could cause harm.

The Buddha does not recommend frivolous speech or gossip, because often it contributes to harm, either because we are speaking about other people behind their back in a negative way, or because gossip can lead to quarrels, misinformation, or the creation of rumours. When we chatter away, what is the purpose? Is it harmless social bonding? Or is there a tinge of pettiness and rancour? The aim of the Buddha is to encourage people to be careful and mindful, and speak words that are truthful, kind, wise and considerate, leading to harmony in society.

RIGHT ACTION

And what, monks, is Right Action? Refraining from taking life, refraining from taking what is not given, refraining from sexual misconduct. This is called Right Action.

Digha Nikaya, 22

Right action will follow from right view, right thought and right speech. Right action is an action that will not cause harm to us or other people. It is an action that will lead to harmony and peace. Here the Buddha presents three Buddhist primary precepts, common to all religions and most societies: do not kill, do not steal, do not have harmful sexual intercourse. The way it is phrased is interesting. We refrain from taking a life – it shows us that in killing we stop a life from living that could have grown over the years. By killing we would not only cause suffering but we would also end a life that could have developed further. Killing is negating the autonomy and the life possibility of that living being.

The Buddha is saying 'do not steal', but even more, that we should use what has been given freely to us. Often we do not feel that we steal, but we might borrow and never return something. Or we might take something by force or by ruse. The Buddha here is looking at our relationship with material goods and how we acquire them. The Buddha in the third precept is not saying that we should never have sexual intercourse, but because it is a powerful desire, we should endeavour not to cause suffering by it, to oneself, to the other person involved, or to someone else. Again, it is looking at desire and seeing how we can work with it in a wise way. We shall look at right livelihood in the chapter on ethics.

RIGHT EFFORT

And what, monks, is Right Effort? Here, monks, a monk rouses his will, makes an effort, stirs up energy, exerts his mind, and strives to prevent the arising of unarisen, evil, unwholesome mental states. He rouses his will ... and strives to overcome evil unwholesome mental states that have arisen. He rouses his will ... and strives to produce unarisen, wholesome mental states. He rouses his will, makes an effort, stirs up energy, exerts his mind, and strives to maintain wholesome mental states that have arisen, not to let them fade away, to bring them to greater growth, to the full perfection of development. This is called Right Effort.

Digha Nikaya, 22

Right effort is divided into four aspects: two aspects deal with things that have not yet happened and the other two consider when certain mental states have arisen. First, the Buddha is urging his disciples to prevent negative states of mind from arising even before they have arisen. How can we do this? It is by becoming more aware of the conditions that give rise to them and of the things that trigger them in the mind. What is it that creates fear, anger, hatred and greed? When are they not there? What helps these negative mental states not to arise? Once more, the Buddha is putting emphasis on awareness and conditionality and here also on prevention. It is easier to deal with negative mental states before they arise. For the Buddha, therefore, it is essential to know the inner and outer conditions that are more likely to give rise to painful mental states and to try to avoid them or to dissolve them. In terms of modern life, we know from experience that tiredness is likely to turn into irritation and anger, so if we rested instead of picking quarrels, it would become easier for ourselves and others. Stress can lead to anxiety: if we try to organise ourselves better or do less, we are less likely to be anxious. If we spend a great deal of time in shopping malls, we are more likely to want things and feel the need to buy them, to feel great frustration and envy if we cannot.

When negative mental states have arisen, one tries to let go of them. Here the first thing to do will be to see these states clearly. It is only by accepting and being fully conscious that negative mental states are happening that one can then know the pain and the perils they cause and so work at letting them go. Anger, envy, jealousy and resentment are painful states of mind. They agitate us and make us feel confined. We will only be able to let go of them once we understand the mechanisms and processes that make them appear.

The Buddha makes us face what is difficult and negative within us, but he is also aware that it is equally important to see and to cultivate what is positive and skilful within us, so the last two efforts deal with wholesome mental states. First we consider how we can cultivate conditions so that wholesome states of mind are more likely to arise. This makes us reflect on the occasions when we are happy, peaceful and contented: what are the conditions that are more likely to give rise to these states of mind, and can we actively cultivate them?

For the Buddha, to cultivate the three trainings of ethics, meditation and wisdom would help us to experience peace and contentment more often. Moreover, he suggests that we can work on and increase positive states of mind once they have arisen. An important thing is to be conscious that they are there. Often we take positive mental states as a given, as our natural condition, so when they are there we take them for granted. However, the Buddha tells us to be fully conscious that they have arisen and to see how we can help them to develop further. Right effort is telling us that we are agents who can have an impact on our states of mind and states of being, and that our fate is not decided in advance.

RIGHT MINDFULNESS

And what, monks, is Right Mindfulness? Here, monks, a monk abides contemplating body as body, ardent, clearly aware and mindful, having put aside hankering and fretting for the world; he abides contemplating feelings as feelings...; he abides contemplating mind as mind...; he abides contemplating mind-objects as mind-objects, ardent, clearly aware, and mindful, having put aside hankering and fretting for the world. This is called Right Mindfulness.

Digha Nikaya, 22

An important aspect of the path is mindfulness. *Sati* in Pali can mean memory or recognition. It is also used as intentness of mind, wakefulness, mindfulness, alertness, lucidity. The Buddha uses it as the skilful paying of attention. One keeps the mind alert to phenomena as they are affecting the body and mind. Right mindfulness is a departure from what was common in ideas about meditation at the time of the Buddha. At that time meditation consisted in trying to create and achieve particular mystical states. But the mindfulness of the Buddha consists instead in being aware of ordinary events that anyone can experience – body, feelings, mind, mind-objects (dhamma). But one is aware of these things in a particular way, impartially, without grasping or rejecting.

In the body one can be aware of the breath, or of specific sensations that might be more apparent, or just of the sensation of contact with the clothes on the body, the air on the cheeks. From this basic awareness of the body many different ways of being mindful of the breath or the body were developed over time. The mindfulness of the feelings looks at agreeable, disagreeable and neutral feelings. The mindfulness of mind is focused on being aware of states of mind and seeing if they are covetous or not, hateful or not, deluded or not, cramped or distracted, developed or undeveloped, concentrated or not, liberated or not.

Mindfulness of mind-objects includes being aware of whether the five hindrances – sensual desire, anger, laziness, restlessness, doubt – are present or not, how they might have arisen, how they can be overcome, how in the future they will not arise any more. One can also be aware of the five constituents of the personality, or of whether the three fires are present or not, or if one of the seven factors of enlightenment – mindfulness, investigation of the dhamma, energy, joy, calm, concentration, equanimity – is present or not, or if one understands and applies the four noble truths or not. Some people translate dhamma in this context as referring to all phenomena and so to the awareness of whatever is happening in any moment of existence. (Right concentration will be dealt with in the practice section.)

THREE CHARACTERISTIC: IMPERMANENCE, SUFFERING, NON-SELF

Whether Buddhas arise in the world or not, it still remains a fact, a firm and necessary condition of existence, that all are impermanent ... that all formations are subject to suffering ... that all things are non-self.

Anguttara Nikaya, III, 134

This is one of the major insights of the Buddha, that things are impermanent, unsatisfactory and have no intrinsic, essential self. Things, people, events are impermanent because they arise and pass away. Nothing stays exactly the same for ever. The fact that things are impermanent does not mean that they change all the time and do not have a certain constancy. The ocean remains relatively the same over time, but its shape can change quite quickly in stormy weather. Mountains are relatively stable, but either they are eroded slowly or they rise slightly with the pushing of the continental plates. People change, moods change, and so on. The ultimate change is death. One of the meditations recommended by the Buddha was cemetery contemplation in order to become fully aware of the impermanence of life.

The statement that 'all formations are subject to suffering' needs to be decoded. *Dukkha* is usually translated as suffering. Some people translate it as stress, others as anguish. In this instance it means two main things: that things are unreliable and unsatisfactory, and this is because they are impermanent. The Buddha saw that suffering arose from the fact that we could not rely entirely on things, on people or on ourselves because of impermanence – an accident, an illness, a shocking event can happen unexpectedly and change any sense of security we might have. Suffering; therefore, can arise because we rely too much on unreliable things. The Buddha is saying that if we know that things are impermanent and unreliable, we will have fewer false expectations and then we can experience less suffering.

Things, people or we ourselves can be considered unsatisfactory in the sense that because of impermanence nothing and no one can give us lasting happiness. We can experience temporary happiness but not the same degree of happiness continuously. We are often looking outside ourselves to find lasting satisfaction in objects, relationships, work, and so on, but they cannot give it to us. The Buddha is suggesting that by understanding unsatisfactoriness we are more likely to experience inner peace and contentment.

The last characteristic is non-self. The Buddha is not saying that there is no self whatsoever but that the self is not what we are looking for and also not what we think it is. In his time this idea was revolutionary, as the main concept was of *atman*, that is either an individual soul or the impersonal supreme, which were then considered either the same or different according to the school of philosophy one believed in. The Buddha, however, saw the idea of *atman* as the problem and as unhelpful. He did not think that there was an intrinsic soul separate from the body or the mind, but that the human being was formed of the five constituents of existence coming together. This is why he says in the next quotation:

'I am' is derivative, not un-derivative. Derivative upon what? Derivative upon form, feeling, perception, formation, and consciousness.
                                        Samyutta Nikaya, XXII, 83

In this quotation the Buddha is telling us that the feeling we have of a separate self that we experience strongly when we are acutely self-conscious is a mirage, that actually this 'I' we feel so strongly about is derivative, is constituted by what forms it. It does not stand on its own. And since the self is not fixed and solid, something can be done about working with it and moulding it in a positive way. The self does not exist in and of itself, it is conditional, it is dependent on what constitutes it.

> *Material form is not self....*
> *Feeling is not self....*
> *Perception is not self....*
> *Formations are not self....*
> *Consciousness is not self....*
> *But is it fitting to regard what is impermanent, unpleasant and subject to change as: this is mine, this is what I am, this is my self?... Seeing thus, bhikkhus, a wise noble disciple becomes dispassionate towards material form, towards feeling, towards perception, towards formations, towards consciousness. As he becomes dispassionate, his lust fades away; with the fading of lust his heart is liberated.'*
>
> Samyutta Nikaya, XXII, 59 (adapted)

Here the Buddha is telling us that the self cannot be reduced to any one of the constituents. Our 'self' cannot be equated just with a bodily experience, or with a feeling or with a perception, or with an intention or with consciousness. Our sense of self derives from the coming together of these five things, which are anyway subject to change and unreliable, so we cannot grasp at any of them as being our 'self'.

The Buddha saw that suffering came upon the grasping and the identification, which fixes us and contracts us around what we grasp at. If we have a looser sense of self as process, then we can relate to the five aggregates in a different way. They form us but we do not need to grasp at them or be defined by them in a reductive way. This will also take away the exaggeration that comes with grasping and identification. If, instead of thinking 'these are my thoughts, my feelings, my problems, my desires' we start to see that a thought has arisen and is impermanent, we can choose to follow it or not according to its skilfulness, instead of what it tells me 'I am' or 'I want'. Then we will feel more freedom in connection with thoughts, feelings and desires.

Chapter Three
*The Community of
Monks and Nuns*

GOING FORTH

And it should be done this way: first the hair and the beard should
be shaved off. Then, after putting on the yellow cloth, the upper robe
should be arranged on one shoulder and homage should be paid at the
bhikkhu's feet. Then kneeling with the hands held out palms together,
this should be said: 'I go for refuge to the Buddha. I go for refuge to
the Dhamma, I go for refuge to the Sangha.... I allow the Going forth
and the Admission to be given by the Triple Refuge.'

Vinaya Mahavagga, Khandhaka 1

At the beginning the way to become a monk was a simple procedure.
As presented in the above quotation, a man shaved his head and beard,
wore some yellow cloth and, kneeling with the palms together, just had to
recite the triple refuge in the presence of the Buddha or an older monk.
Shaving the hair and beard was a sign of renunciation but also a way
to recognise each other as a group and for lay people to recognise the
Buddhist monastics. In Thailand at the turn of the twentieth century when
thieves impersonated monks to receive free food, the monks had to shave
their eyebrows to look different from these false monks.

Cutting the hair and beard was to help the monks let go of certain habits of adornment; at the same time it simplified their life. If they shaved their head and face, they did not need shampoo or fragrant oil. They did not have to worry about their hair not being luxurious enough and did not have to compare their hairdo with that of other men. They renounced something they were used to – looking a certain way – and at the same time renunciation made it easier for them to be renunciants.

Kneeling with the palms of the hands together as in prayer is a common religious act. It implies humility and surrender. By putting oneself in a lower position, one acknowledges that one is ready to learn and to be taught. By putting the palms together one is assuming a non-threatening position, both hands being within sight. Some people suggest that it also means that one brings all of oneself into that act: all of one's body, heart and mind.

Taking refuge in the triple gems – Buddha, Dhamma, Sangha – is the main way for monastics, but also for lay people, to enter formally the Buddhist path. Taking refuge in the Buddha means that one puts one's trust in the Buddha and his accomplishments. It also means that one believes that one can become a Buddha, has the same potential as the Buddha for awakening. In Korean meditation halls, if there is no Buddha statue in the hall, in the morning and in the evening the monks or the nuns bow to each other, and in doing so they bow to their own potential of Buddhahood. They remind each other that each of them is trying to cultivate and experience the same awakening as the Buddha's.

Taking refuge in the Dhamma means that the monks have faith in the teachings of the Buddha and also that it can be a foundation and support for their life. By cultivating the Dhamma they aim to develop their potential and be of benefit to everyone. This refuge means that they understand the teachings and plan to apply them. Taking refuge in the Sangha (community) means that one cannot do this alone; it is easier if one is with other people who have the same intention. The community is there to support the individual but also to act as an inspiration. One respects the community and is also part of that community. Each person is essential for the community to exist but also for the dhamma to be practised and for the Buddha's message to be transmitted over time. In certain traditions, such as Japanese Soto Zen, there is a chant in which one takes refuge, honouring and naming all the great masters of the past. It is a way to remember where the dhamma comes from and how it has reached us. In the triple refuge the Buddha shows that merely following one of the refuges is not enough. All three are complementary – again the Buddha presents a pluralist and complex view of what it means to enter and walk the path.

Over time becoming a monk became a little more elaborate. At first the Buddha merely had to say 'Come, monk' for a man to join his group of renunciates and then shave and put on the yellow robe. After the Buddha's death, the tradition of ordination in two sequences was developed. First there was the 'going forth', in which the young monk, who needed to be at least eight years old, took the ten precepts from a preceptor and a master. Later there was the full ordination, when the young novice took 227 precepts in front of ten elders. Nowadays there are variations in the age of 'going forth', in numbers of precepts, in the receiving of full ordination, and in the ceremonies of ordination – some are more complex than others.

The 227 precepts are found in the *Patimokkha,* a text that resumes the code of discipline. This text was, and still is, recited at full moon and new moon day by the monastics. There need to be at least four monastics to do this properly. This text is part of the *Vinaya* (literally discipline), a Buddhist scripture from which most of the quotations for this chapter are taken. The *Vinaya* contains all the precepts, the codes of behaviour, all the commentaries and the stories associated with the establishment of the precepts. In English translation it comes to six volumes.

At the beginning there were no precepts, but as more and more people joined the community, mistakes were made and so each time there was a problem caused by a certain type of behaviour, the Buddha set up a rule. At times, too, lay people came to the Buddha complaining of the behaviour of some monks and the Buddha would set up a rule. The first precepts dealt with sexual behaviour and the Buddha decided that monks should not engage in any sexual activities. Thus normally Buddhist monks are celibate, though this has changed more recently in some countries and some schools do not follow this rule.

The ethical code set by the Buddha for the monk was situational in that it responded to specific circumstances at specific times and places, and then was applied to all monastics. At the time of his death the Buddha suggested to Ananda that the minor rules could be abolished and that the monks had only to keep the major ones. Traditionally, however, it is thought that because Ananda did not ask precisely which minor precepts the Buddha meant, then all were kept just in case. It looks as though the

Buddha understood that because the rules arose out of a certain conditioned environment, some might not be adaptable to future times. Even so, in the traditions that followed his death it seems to have been thought more prudent to retain all the rules. Later, some rules were ignored or fell in abeyance as they did not fit the mores of the times.

> *Nanda, it is not proper for you, a clansman who has gone forth out of faith from the home life into homelessness, to put on pressed and ironed robes, anoint your eyes and take a glazed bowl. What is proper for you, a clansman who has gone forth out of faith from the home life into homelessness, is to be a forest dweller, an eater only of alms food got by begging a wearer of refuse-rag robes, and to dwell without regard for sensual desires.*
>
> Samyutta Nikaya, XXI, 8

Nanda was a half-brother of the Buddha. The Buddha is reputed to have convinced him to become a monk somewhat against Nanda's wishes. It took him some time to feel that this life of renunciation was for him. Although he seemed to have kept the rules, it appears he could not stop himself from wanting to look his best and use some adornments, and to have a fancy bowl. Here the Buddha reminds him that the intention of the monastics is to go beyond any sensual desires, to endeavour to want nothing and to use very little, to simplify one's life to the maximum.

This was not easy for some of the young men who joined the Buddha. Many came from wealthy families and were used to more comfort and to keeping certain standards. Many of the rules about food and adornments were to act as a reminder of the life these young men had chosen and to help them go beyond certain habits of ease and embellishments. Moreover, lay people had to be able to look up to them as being representative of a simpler way of life. The various spiritual groups of that time were judged on their level of austerities, and since the Buddha did not want to outdo others in austerities because of the middle way, his monks had to behave correctly in terms of simplicity and renunciation. As for practice, the Buddha encouraged his monks to reduce their wants so that they would have fewer needs.

THE NUNS

'Lord, are women capable, after going forth from home life into homelessness in the Dhamma and Discipline declared by the Buddha, of realizing the fruit of Stream Entry or Once-Return or Non-Return or Arahantship?' 'They are, Ananda.'

Vinaya Mahavagga, Khandhaka 110

This episode occurred about five years after the Buddha's awakening, when Mahapajapati, the Buddha's aunt and foster-mother, had repeatedly asked him to ordain her like the monks. The Buddha seemed quite reluctant, as nobody else had done this before, and renunciants were males up to that point. To solve the dilemma, Ananda, who throughout the suttas is shown as a great supporter of the nuns, asked the Buddha if he thought that women could attain the end of the path – awakening. The Buddha replied in the affirmative, which was quite revolutionary for his time, 500 BCE, whereas in 1000 CE some people in Europe were still wondering if women even had a soul like men.

The Buddha is saying that women can attain the four stages of awakening (mentioned in the first chapter) in the same way as men. Each stage is viewed within the framework of past and future lives, which was a common belief of his time. By attaining the first stage, the one where beliefs in self, rites and rituals are lost, and doubt disappears, a person is said to have achieved 'stream entry'. The Buddha declared that such a person would only be reborn at the most seven times more and not in any painful destinations like the various hells. Such a person was said to understand the dhamma well and lead an impeccably ethical life.

Whoever attained the second stage, where greed and hatred were weakened, was said to have to be born only once more and then to be assured of awakening in that next life. In the third stage, where greed and hatred are dissolved, the person will not be reborn as a human but only once or twice in the heavens and attain awakening there. At the arahant stage, where conceit, restlessness and ignorance disappear, the person is fully awakened and will not be reborn again anywhere. The Buddha in this passage is saying that women and men are equal in terms of awakening and in what they can achieve through Buddhist practice. When the Buddha accepted women in his community of monastics at the urging of Ananda and the supplications of his aunt, he was purported to have given them eight conditions, which seem to have been devised to protect the nuns, to avoid upsetting the patriarchal supremacy of the monks, and to appease the lay people and supporters who might have been shocked by this revolutionary move.

One condition was for the nuns not to live far away from a group of monks. In the *Vinaya* texts various episodes are related of attacks on the nuns when they practised in the forests on their own. In India any unmarried or single woman living apart from her family was frequently accused of leading a loose life and was often preyed upon and attacked. Once the nuns were seen as under the protection of a group of monks and living nearer to a town, they were more likely to be left in peace. A separate set of rules was devised for the nuns over time, but they have many more than the monks – from 290 to 356 (over time, different sets of rules with minor changes were elaborated by different traditions). Scholars think that the nuns' precepts are made from a combination of the monks precepts applicable to women plus the ones that arose from mistakes made by nuns in the Buddha's lifetime.

At the time of the Buddha many women joined the community and had great attainments. Some of their accomplishments are recorded in the *Therigatha (Verses of the Nuns),* a collection of seventy-three poems. This one is by Mitta, a Sakyan woman, who joined Mahapajapati with the first group of women who went to ask the Buddha to ordain them:

> *To be reborn among the gods*
> *I fasted and fasted*
> *every two weeks,*
> *day eight, fourteen, fifteen*
> *and a special day.*
>
> *Now with a shaved head*
> *and Buddhist robes*
> *I eat one meal a day.*
> *I don't long to be a god.*
> *There is no fear in my heart.*

This poem is interesting because it shows how Mitta moved from traditional brahminical rituals to becoming a nun and practising the Buddha's teachings. She went from a metaphysical (other life) aspiration – to be reborn in a god's realm – to a psycho-spiritual (this life) experience – not to have any fear in her heart any more. The Buddha was breaking away from tradition and offering something practical that could be tested and experienced in one's lifetime. Even if it included in its theology a multiple-lives format, the attainment was in this life.

> *I should like to provide the Community with rains cloth for as long as I live. And I should like similarly to provide food for visitors, food for those setting out on a journey, food for the sick, and food for the sick-attendants; and I should like similarly to provide medicine, and a constant supply of gruel; and I should like similarly to provide bathing cloths for the Community of bhikkhunis.*
>
> *Vinaya Mahavagga, Khandhaka 18*

This was proposed by Ambapali, a courtesan of Vesali, which was the capital of the Licchavis. The episode happened some weeks before the Buddha died, when he was visiting this region. Ambapali came to hear him speak and she was so moved by his teaching that she made this offering among many others. She presented the kind of things that a layperson could give to the community to support its members. The Buddha allowed the monks and nuns to be given and use what he called the four requisites: food, shelter, clothes and medicines.

'Rains cloth' is a special bathing cloth used by monks residing in monasteries that is donated at the beginning of the rain retreats. Ambapali also wanted to offer special bathing cloths for nuns. When monastics washed, they had to do so in a well-concealed way, so that their naked body could not be seen by anyone. The monks had the official triple robes: a sarong, an outer robe and a shoulder cloth, plus this special bathing cloth. The nuns had five robes, the same first three as the monks plus a vest or bodice and a bath cloth.

Ambapali became a nun herself later and one of her poems is in the *Therigatha*. In this long poem, of which I shall present just the last two verses, she shows her understanding of impermanence in reference to her body, which was known to be very beautiful. She also seems to have had some sense of humour:

> *My feet were beautiful,*
> *delicate as if filled with cotton.*
> *Now because of old age*
> *they are cracked and rotten.*
> *This is the teaching of one who speaks the truth.*

This is how my body was.
Now it is dilapidated,
the place of pain,
an old house
with the plaster falling off.

By allowing women to join his community, the Buddha gave them a place equal spiritually to that of the men. It also provided a way for the women, left by their husbands to become monks, not to be left on their own to lead a difficult single life but to join a community of women and to cultivate, practise and develop their own potential for awakening, wisdom and compassion.

DEALING WITH OFFENCES

Now bhikkhus who know the gravity of schism in the community should
not suspend that bhikkhu as long as he does not see his offence, if
they judge thus: 'He is learned and desirous of training; if we suspend
him without his seeing his offence, we shall not be able to keep the
Uposatha observance with him, or the Pavarana ceremony (invitation to
criticize) at the end of the Rains, or carry out acts of the Community,
or sit on the same seat, or share gruel, or share the refectory, or live
under the same roof, or perform acts of respect to elders, with him;
we shall do these things without him, and because of that there will be
quarrelling, brawling, wrangling, disputing, and eventually schism, division
and dissenting acts in the community.'

Vinaya Mahavagga, Khandhaka 110

This was said during an episode where there had been a misunderstanding between two monks. One monk did something that the other monk thought was an offence, but because the first monk did not know it was an offence and so did it unintentionally, he was left with the impression that it was not an offence. So the first monk did not think that he had committed a fault, while the other did. Both were learned and respected monks with supporters, and after rumours circulated for a while amongst the two groups, one group decided to suspend the offender unilaterally. This started to create a schism in the community. Finally the Buddha was told about this discord and decided to intervene. He went to talk to each group. First the Buddha suggested that they needed to have further discussion with the monk. This would enable the monk to understand his offence, then he would be able to confess it; after which, everybody could move on and resume living in harmony.

The Buddha was very concerned that there should be a harmonious relationship between the members of his community. He repeatedly stressed the importance of living in harmony and dissolving dissension. The last of the five major offences, which can cause a monk to be excluded from the community, is creating a schism. In order to create good conditions for the fostering of harmony, the Buddha created a ceremony called 'Pavarana', which literally means invitation. Each monk 'invited' other monks to point out his faults. This ceremony happened at the end of the three-month rain retreat, which occurred on the full moon in October. The monastics gathered all together and related to each other what they had done, seen, heard or suspected that might have been a breaking of certain rules or the committing of certain offences. The Buddha created this ceremony in order to help the monks or nuns live more peacefully together and to give them an opportunity to atone for their mistakes. Moreover, it was a way for them to remind one another of the rules.

The Buddha seemed to recognise that it might be difficult for a group of people to live together for three months in close proximity. He therefore created a ceremony in which monks or nuns could become more aware of what they had done wrong during the retreat. It was a way to reflect on one's past actions and their consequences, and to have the opportunity to ask for admonishments or instructions. This ceremony of invitation encouraged people to become more aware of what they were doing. Having the intention to be aware might not be enough, as it was hard to break certain habits, so listening from others about it would help. Moreover, sometimes one might think that one had acted in a way that was proper and harmless, while it was not. The ceremony was not set up to be a litany of accusations, but the aim was for every person to reflect on their conduct and to see if they helped foster harmony or not, if they were selfish or not, if they were mindful or not. The principle was based on the intention to work with the difficulty. By becoming more conscious of one's mistakes, one could work more on them with the help of the whole community. This was based on the belief that everyone was fallible and at the same time that everyone had the potential to change.

The Uposatha day is a special day for the Buddhist monastics and lay people, a day dedicated to the Dhamma. The name is derived from a brahmanical ceremony where certain ascetics taught groups of people at the times of the full and new moon. The Buddha decided to use the same days, plus the two quarter-moon days. In this way four times a month there would be a special Dhamma day for the whole community. This day seems to have been created at the suggestion of King Bimbisara. On Uposatha day the monastics generally gave talks to the lay people while the lay people kept the eight precepts. It was also the day chosen for the recitation of the monastic rules, but this was done only every second Uposatha day and only if there were more than four monks or nuns. Before reciting the precepts, monks or nuns would confess any breach of the rules to each other.

> *But since you see your transgression as such and so act in accordance with the Dhamma, we forgive it; for it is growth in the Noble Ones' Discipline when a man sees a transgression as such and so acts in accordance with the Dhamma and enters upon restraint in the future.*
>
> Vinaya Mahavagga, Khandhaka 17

The Buddha does not believe that a person is born bad and fated to make mistakes; he trusts that a person can make amends and can change his or her behaviour. This is why he puts so much emphasis on confession and self-reflection. One needs a certain level of awareness to see the causes and consequences of one's action. One also needs to forgive so that the person can move on and have the faith that they are not essentially bad, that they can help themselves and use restraint in the future. For the Buddha it is essential to see the harm caused to oneself or to others and to have the intention not to cause such harm again.

The Buddha put great emphasis on being conscious of what one thought, said or did, and the effect of these thoughts, words and acts. There are two terms he used often: *sati* and *sampajanna*, which are nearly synonymous. You can also put them together as *satisampajanna*. *Sati*, as we have seen in the section of the second chapter on right mindfulness, means consciousness of something, but it can also mean memory and recognition. For the Buddha it is important to have in memory the intention of harmlessness and the intention of restraint. One recognises the causes and conditions that lead to harm; by remembering these, one knows what is unskilful and so cultivates restraint and acts accordingly.

Sampajanna means clear apprehension of oneself in all aspects of the moment. It is the ability to have a clear perception of one's behaviour and actions. In the texts, one finds four types of clear comprehension: one is associated with one's goal, one with meditation, one with absence of illusion, and one with what is appropriate, what is proper. In this quotation the Buddha is referring to the last type: he thinks that it is essential to know what is skilful, what is ethical, what is in accordance with living in a community or relating to lay people. So one's actions and words are not just based on what one wants but on what is appropriate for the whole community, what is beneficial for them. One will therefore have to restrain certain desires and automatic habits for the sake of the greater community, but also because one knows that it will be beneficial for each individual, who is also part of that community.

CARING FOR EACH OTHER

Bhikkhus, you have neither mother nor father to look after you. If you do not look after each other, who will look after you? Let him who would look after me look after one who is sick. If he has a preceptor, his preceptor should, as long as he lives, look after him until his recovery. His teacher, if he has one, should do likewise. Or his co-resident, or his pupil, or one who has the same preceptor, or one who has the same teacher. If he has none of these, the Community should look after him. Not to do so is an offence of wrongdoing.

Vinaya Mahavagga, Khandhaka 18

The Buddha said these words on the occasion when a monk, ill with dysentery, had not been looked after by the other monks. When he realised the monk was ill and unattended, the Buddha himself went to take care of him with his attendant. When he had rebuked them, the monks had said that they had not taken care of the sick monk because he had not done anything for them. Here the Buddha is pointing out to the monks that although they are individuals, not linked together necessarily by any special bonds, they need to look after one another. They have to care for one another as if they are part of the same family. He wants the community to function as a family, which takes care of their members out of kindness, concern and a sense of connection, irrespective of any difficulties or any tangible reciprocity.

The Buddha points out that you cannot wait for people to do something for you before you do something for them. As soon as they enter the community, members need to feel connected to one another and to be responsible for one another. Each member has to see the other as the Buddha himself. If the Buddha were sick they would take care of him, and in the same way they should take care of any of the monastics, irrespective of their past actions or non-actions. In this passage the Buddha also showed the line of relationships and the important people in the life of a monk or a nun, a tradition that has existed to this day in Buddhist monasteries and nunneries.

First one has a preceptor, who is considered like one's father or mother. In Korea, the preceptor and the preceptress have been ordained for some years and might be an abbot or an abbess of a small temple. They undertake to look after a novice, to be responsible for him or her when the novice receives the precepts. They will give him or her monastic clothes and will take care of the young monk or nun's needs. One can also have a teacher – a meditation master, a Dhamma scholar or a precept master – who can be a guide on the Buddhist path. The preceptors/preceptresses or teachers will have other disciples and share life with them, becoming like siblings or uncles/aunts, depending on their age and position. Disciples feel more connected to them and will be helped by them in times of need. If, however, circumstances are such that a disciple does not have a specific Dhamma family, the Buddha is very clear that the whole community then must feel concerned for the well-being of the individual.

> *Venerable sir, as to that, whichever of us returns first from the village with almsfood prepares the seats, sets out the water for drinking and for washing and puts the refuse bucket in its place. Whichever of us returns last eats any food left over, if he wishes; otherwise he throws it away where there is no greenery or drops it into water where there is no life. He puts away the seats and the water for drinking and for washing. He puts away the refuse bucket after washing it, and he sweeps out the refectory. Whoever notices that the pots of water for drinking washing or the latrine are low or empty takes care of them. If they are too heavy for him, he calls someone else by a signal of the hand and they move it by joining hands, but because of this we do not break out into speech. But every five days we sit together all night discussing the Dhamma. That is how we abide diligent, ardent and resolute.*

> *Majjhima Nikaya, 128*

This quotation shows how the monks or nuns lived harmoniously. Each of them knew what to do and intended to do it, and so little speech was needed. At the time of the Buddha, the monks and the nuns went once a day begging for alms in the morning. The rule was that there was no eating of food after midday and no keeping of food overnight. The monks and nuns therefore generally had to live not too far from lay people in order to be able to receive food. This is why their monasteries and nunneries were often situated near villages or urban centres. The Buddha did not want his disciples to lead reclusive lives far away from ordinary life. He wanted his monastics to live in a reciprocal relationship with the Buddhist lay people.

Because the monastics could not keep food overnight, they ate and shared what they could. What was left was disposed of in such manner as not to cause damage either to plants or to animals. Here again, the Buddha is emphasising harmlessness and awareness of one's environment. The monastics shared the tasks of gathering water, washing the bowls, and so on. There is an understanding that each of them will try to do something with good will and without checking who has done more or less. The various tasks, carried out while they are eating and obtaining food, are accomplished with care and concern as part of the practice, a component of the cultivation of the eightfold path.

The Buddha was keen that his monastics should not spend time in idle chatter. This enabled them to develop a way of life which was respectful and in which they understood each other without the need for a great deal of talking. The Buddha's disciples were noted for their calmness and silence. There are several episodes recounted where people think that the Buddha is not there because his presence is so silent. At special times, however, they would gather with the specific aim of talking, sharing their experiences, discussing the fine points of the Dhamma as taught by the Buddha or as demonstrated by the elders.

AN ETHICAL LIFE

He abstains from injuring seeds and plants. He practises eating only in one part of the day, abstaining from eating at night and outside the proper time. He abstains from dancing, singing, music, and theatrical shows. He abstains from wearing garlands, smartening himself with scents, and embellishing himself with unguents. He abstains from high and large couches. He abstains from accepting gold and silver. He abstains from accepting raw grain. He abstains from accepting raw meat. He abstains from accepting women and girls. He abstains from accepting men and women slaves. He abstains from accepting goats and sheep. He abstains from accepting fowl and pigs. He abstains from accepting elephants, cattle, horses and mares. He abstains from accepting fields and land. He abstains from going on errands and running messages. He abstains from buying and selling. He abstains from false weights, false metal and false measures. He abstains from cheating, deceiving, defrauding and trickery. He abstains from wounding, murdering, binding, brigandage, plunder, and violence.

Majjhima Nikaya, 27

In this passage the Buddha is listing some of the rules that the Buddhist monastics are expected to follow. Here again, as is characteristic of the Buddha, the main emphasis is on harmlessness and simplicity. The first part of this quotation is about what a monk should not do. He is not supposed to till the land as he is forbidden to deal with grain and plants. He eats modestly once a day, so he is not constantly going off to beg for food. Lay people are expected to give him food only once a day. Because he is intent on awakening, he does not need anything that is going to distract him from that goal. Furthermore, if he is going to various spectacles, he is more likely to be tempted and lured by his desires. If he is engaged in singing, he might get overexcited or lose himself in the music. Nor does he need to embellish himself. He needs to keep things to a simple minimum. Large and high couches were a symbol of riches and power, so the Buddha wanted his monks to be humble and not to compete with each other in getting a higher bed.

The next part is about what the monk should not accept. It is very likely that this was decided after lay people gave certain things to monks, and the Buddha thought that it would not be suitable or conducive to cultivating harmlessness and simplicity. First, a monk is not supposed to handle money, and especially not to hoard any. So his relationship with lay people is not of a mercenary nature. They must give a monk only what he needs to eat that day as he cannot keep anything overnight. There is no risk of accumulation. If he were to take raw grain, he would have to have land in which to plant and cultivate it. If he were to sell it to a farmer he would engage in a monetary exchange, which is forbidden.

He must not accept raw meat because it would mean that it had been killed recently for the purpose of feeding the monk and that is forbidden. Furthermore, the monk depends entirely on lay people for his food, for he has no way to cook anything (things changed over time about having no way to cook).

The monk is celibate, so there is no point in giving him women and anyway he has to guard his senses. He cannot have slaves, which means that he must clean, sweep and do all the ordinary tasks himself. This must have been a shock for men coming from a wealthy background. It is still a shock nowadays to young men who have been cosseted at home. Again, he is not a farmer and depends on others for his sustenance, so he does not need to be given farm animals. He is not going to engage in any trade and therefore does not need beasts of burden. He does not need money, so he does not need animals or grain as his bank account. A monk is not supposed to own anything apart from the things that help him to satisfy the four basic needs – a bowl, some cloth, some medicines, and some temporary shelter during the rains. Throughout his life various gardens were given to the Buddha so that he could pass the rains retreat with his monks, but the garden belonged to the whole community and not to one individual.

Monks have to abstain from running errands, and especially from acting as a go-between to set up a proposal of marriage. The monk is supposed not even to officiate formally at a marriage. The only thing that a monk can do is bless the married couple after the official ceremony. The monk is not supposed to act as a go-between for anybody. He must not get involved in the world of desires in any way. He needs to be impartial and to remain above the fray. He cannot engage in any commercial enterprise even if it is an honest one, and particularly if it is a dishonest one. He cannot harm people in any way, so he must have nothing to do with war or violence.

All in all therefore; Buddhist monastics could not do much apart from studying, following the rules, meditating and teaching. It was an existence taken to its bare minimum, though not espousing complete self-denial, since it was in the cultivation of the middle way.

Bhikkhus, a bhikkhu is fit to go on a mission when he has eight qualities. What are the eight? Here a bhikkhu is one who listens, who gets others to listen, who learns, who remembers, who recognises, who gets others to recognise, who is skilled in the consistent and the inconsistent, and who does not make trouble.

Vinaya Mahavagga, Khandhaka 17

For the first five years the young monks were supposed to stay with the community and their elders in order to learn, study and meditate. After five years the monastics could leave the community to wander and benefit others, but they had to have eight qualities. The fact that the monks were encouraged not to spend so much time in idle chatter or gossip meant that when they talked, they talked more mindfully, but also that they were able to listen with more mindfulness. Listening well is a quality admired and encouraged by the Buddha, alongside knowing how to make others listen. People will listen more easily if one speaks in a calm and clear way, speaking neither too much nor too little, again the middle way.

The Buddha puts great emphasis on learning and cultivating. Being a monk is not about achieving a certain status and a certain respect in society, but about developing the person as much as one can. One is not fixed and solid. One can always learn more, develop more wisdom and compassion. The monk who can go on a mission is someone who remembers. He remembers the precepts, he remembers his aspiration for wisdom and compassion, and he remembers to act skilfully and appropriately. At all times he remembers that he is a monk and as such needs to follow a certain line of conduct.

Before sharing the dhamma with others, the monk or nun needs to understand each teaching and at the same time be able to explain it so that the person listening can understand it well and apply it easily. The Buddha is interested in what is relevant and essential, and he wants his followers to do the same. He does not want his disciples to become lost in irrelevance. He wants them to be committed to the path and its practice to the exclusion of anything else. In this way the practice of the disciples will have an effect on them and then they will be able to share this with others.

The Buddha does not want his monks and nuns to cause trouble of any kind. There is enough suffering in the world: why should they add to it? This is why his monastics need to practise diligently and intensely before leaving and sharing what they have learnt with others. These eight qualities were attributed to Sariputta by the Buddha, who thought that Sariputta was capable of going forth in order to meet people and talk to them about the teachings of the Buddha in a beneficial way.

Chapter Four

Practice

THE FIVE HINDRANCES

But the Tathagata is aware that whosoever has been emancipated, is now emancipated or will be emancipated from the world; all these will do so by removing the five hindrances that defile the mind and weaken understanding, by firmly establishing their minds in the four foundations of mindfulness, and by cultivating the seven factors of enlightenment in their true nature.

Anguttara Nikaya, X, 95

The five hindrances are sensual desires, ill-will, torpor, restlessness and sceptical doubt. The Buddha compared the effects of sensual desires to colours swirling in a bowl of water. The water being tainted by the colours, one would not be able to see one's face clearly on the surface of the water. In the same way, when we are submerged by sensual desires, our whole body and mind is suffused by attraction and lust, and it is hard to see clearly. The analogy for ill-will is that of the water in the bowl: when it is heated over a fire, bubbles and boils, one would again be unable to see one's face clearly in the water. In a similar manner, ill-will agitates us and causes us to act in a blind, aggressive and destructive way.

Torpor is compared to water being covered over with plants and algae, so that one cannot see anything and the water loses its reflective quality. Similarly, if we are assailed by laziness and sloth, we cannot think of doing anything, we cannot act and behave decisively and compassionately. Worry and restlessness are compared to the water being disturbed by a strong wind, so that the surface has too many ripples for anyone to see any reflection. Again, when we are restless and worried, our mind goes round in circles and our body is agitated, which does not help us to see and think clearly. The final hindrance, sceptical doubt, is compared to muddy and opaque water, which would also prevent seeing one's face clearly on the surface of the water. In like manner, sceptical doubt would muddle our mind and stop us from seeing what is skilful and unskilful, and from acting accordingly.

Reflecting on these comparisons, we can see that the Buddha is an astute observer of the mind and body and what afflicts them. If we are too lost in sensual desires, we are caught in our immediate reactions to what we encounter and it is very difficult to see the negative consequences of acting on these desires. Since sluggishness is very paralysing and feeds upon itself, the Buddha wanted his disciples to be active and creative, and to help themselves to be so. Malice or the desire to hurt is completely anathema to the Buddha's ideas of harm-lessness and compassion. These hindrances are also painful personally: to be plagued by worry, agitation and regrets can create a great deal of stress. Wavering, hesitation and indecision will cause suffering not only to us but also to others.

To counteract the powers of the five hindrances, the Buddha suggested the cultivation of mindfulness in four ways – body (*kaya*), sensations (*vedana*), mind (*citta*), mental objects (*dhamma*). What is interesting about the Buddha is that he did not dissociate body and mind in terms of what one is mindful of. *Kaya* means a group or body of something, and so the reference to *rupa* (body) *kaya* here signifies physical body. *Vedana* refers to what we know through the senses, which includes bodily sensations and mental sensations, which are then divided into pleasant, unpleasant, neutral. *Citta* refers to mental factors and consciousness, including states of mind affected by feelings, perceptions and intentions. *Dhamma* used in the plural, as here in this classification, includes mental and bodily phenomena, transitory elements of experience and the different things that constitute elements of existence – various conditions, conceptions and ideas. The Buddha, therefore, wanted his disciples to be as aware of their inner world as of the outer world and to see how these two worlds interacted, influenced and conditioned each other.

To help his disciples achieve awakening, the Buddha put great emphasis on the development of seven qualities, called the seven factors of enlightenment – mindfulness, investigation, energy, joy, tranquillity, concentration and equanimity. Investigation is the detailed study of the teachings of the Buddha, but it is also a detailed examination of objects, physical and mental phenomena, everything that is composite and conditioned. Energy, effort, perseverance are essential qualities to apply in order to advance on the Buddhist path, otherwise one would not go anywhere. For the Buddha one has to act and do something. Even meditation, which looks like a motionless activity, requires great energy and dedication, which are both essential.

The Buddha realised that it is necessary to experience joy, interest, enthusiasm and delight on the path, otherwise we will not continue. The path will bring us joy and at the same we need to cultivate joy to develop the path. This is not merely a physical joy of lightness and good humour, but also a mental joy infused with contentment and happiness – to be doing the right thing at the right time, to feel stable, open and creative. Tranquillity again is something to cultivate and something that will also be the result of the practice. It is the ability we have to be at rest, at peace, calm in mind and body.

Concentration is the focusing one does in meditation and at the same time it is the state of composure, which will be developed by that exercise. It helps the mind to be more spacious and stable. This term can also refer to certain deep states of absorption in meditation that the Buddha experienced and were a common interest of the Indian practitioners of the various spiritual groups of his time. Equanimity refers to a certain type of serenity and equilibrium one is trying to cultivate and which will also be developed over time. It is not indifference, nor does it lead one to feel separate from people and things; rather, it is the way one meets things and people with impartiality and equality. It gives stability, making one less vulnerable to the tumultuous quality of life. It helps one to be less afraid and more creatively engaged. It enables one to become less perturbed and thus more responsive in a wise and compassionate way.

MINDFULNESS

All things have desire for their roots, attention provides their being, contact their origin, feeling their meeting-place, concentration confrontation with

them, mindfulness control of them, understanding is the highest of them,
and deliverance is their core.

Anguttara Nikaya, VIII, 83

Here the Buddha defines the problems and the solution as he saw them.
As we go about our life, we come into contact with different things in
the world – sights, sounds, smells, and so on. For example, one minute
we do not see something, then it appears in our field of vision. As we
pay attention to it, we come into contact with it, be it a beautiful flower,
a sweet perfume, a great house or some ugly rubbish. This contact will
give rise to certain feelings of likes or dislikes, which in turn will give rise
to desires – I want this or I hate that.

Concentration enables us to stop the process by which desire arises, by
breaking the link between contact and feeling. By developing our capacity to
focus directly on what happens when we come in contact with something,
we are not caught in the mechanism of desire, but become freer from our
automatic reactions of wanting and rejecting. Mindfulness creates a space and
makes us see the composite and conditioned nature of experience. When
we are mindful, we see things clearly as they arise and they happen to
be, and then we are able to reflect and respond creatively without being
blinded by desires or feelings.

Here, Ananda, for the Tathagata feelings are known as they arise, as
they are present, as they disappear; perceptions are known as they arise,
as they are present, as they disappear; thoughts are known as they arise,
as they are present, as they disappear.

Majjhima Nikaya, 123

Mindfulness means that we are aware of ourselves and of the impact of
the world on us in a complete way. Like the Buddha, we try to see and
know when feelings begin, how long they last and when they disappear,
both with perceptions and with thoughts.

To be able to experience the transiency of feelings, perceptions and
thoughts is a revelation. We have a tendency to 'fix ourselves' – I am a
happy person, I am an angry person. But happiness and anger are not fixed
and solid, they come upon conditions and disappear upon other conditions.
It is quite freeing to see that. It is the same with perceptions. When we
perceive something, we have a tendency to fix and solidify what we perceive

and our perceptions of it. Thoughts that are very transient can also feel very solid and heavy. The Buddha is trying to make people be aware in their actual experience of how feelings, perceptions and thoughts arise, stay a while and pass away. When one becomes more aware and conscious of the changing nature of things, it become easier to deal with them

A bhikkhu should abide contemplating the body as a body, ardent, fully aware, and mindful, having put away covetousness and grief for the world. Or he should abide contemplating feelings as feelings, ardent, fully aware, and mindful, having put away covetousness and grief for the world. Or he should abide contemplating consciousness as consciousness, ardent, fully aware, and mindful, having put away covetousness and grief for the world. Or he should abide contemplating mental objects as mental objects, ardent, fully aware, and mindful, having put away covetousness and grief for the world.

Samyutta Nikaya, XLVII, 18, 43

The Buddha encouraged his disciples to develop a mindfulness that is non-judgemental, without greed or hate, and that is also energetic and keen. Its aim is to bring a benign and alert eye to our whole experience. Here he presented the four foundations of mindfulness more precisely. One starts with becoming more aware of the body, and the Buddha suggested various ways of doing this. One can be aware of the in-breath and the out-breath. One can be mindful of the four postures – sitting, standing, walking and lying down. This brings about an awareness and presence of mind and a clear comprehension of the body. A person becomes clearly and fully aware of coming and going, looking, eating and so on. Then one pays attention to the various bodily parts from the top of the head down to the soles of the feet. Next, one looks at the four elements that the Buddha thought constituted the body – air, water, fire and earth. Then the Buddha recommended his monks and nuns to go to charnel grounds and observe the decomposition of the various cadavers. In India the bodies are generally burned in special open areas on top of wood pyres. The Buddha thought that this would help his disciples see for themselves the impermanent nature of the body and give rise to more urgency for the practice.

In terms of being aware of feelings and sensations, the Buddha recommended being aware of pleasant, unpleasant and neutral feelings. He suggested that one should become aware of whether the feelings and sensations were more worldly or unworldly in connection with pleasant, unpleasant or neutral feeling-tones of sensation. The Buddha wanted students to be more conscious of the basic tonality of their existence and how this affected them, even before the tonality itself gave rise to happiness or unhappiness. If we experience a pleasant sensation, automatically we will want it to continue or to repeat itself in exactly the same way. The Buddha was trying to make people more aware of pleasant and unpleasant sensations as they happen and to see more clearly that they are conditional and changing.

In terms of mind and consciousness, the Buddha encouraged his disciples to be aware of whether or not their minds were affected by lust, hatred or delusion, contraction or distraction, and of whether or not they felt exalted, concentrated or liberated. To be aware of mental objects is to be aware of whether one's mind is affected or not by one of the five hindrances – sensual desires, ill-will, torpor, restlessness and sceptical doubt. Furthermore, it is important to be mindful of the five aggregates, the six bases (eyes, visual forms and the contact between the two; ears, sounds and the contact between the two, and so on), the seven factors of awakening and the four noble truths. Again we see the teachings of the Buddha as looking deeply into all aspects of our existence. The Buddha seems to have been a psychologist and phenomenologist ahead of his times.

MINDFULNESS OF THE BREATH

Mindfulness of the breath should be maintained for the purpose of cutting off discursive thoughts...
Mean thoughts, trivial thoughts
come tempting the mind and fly away;
not understanding these thoughts in the mind,
the heart strays chasing them back and forth.
A man understanding these thoughts in his mind
expels them with vigorous mindfulness.
And one enlightened has done with them all;
for no more temptation then stirs his mind.

Udana, IV, 1

The Buddha was not fatalistic, he believed in human agency. When, for example, he told his monks and nuns to be mindful of the breath, it was for a definite purpose, to make their mind clearer and lighter. Thoughts generally appear and we follow them here and there. The more we think them in a distracted way, the more we will amplify them and give them free rein. This will reach the point where we feel that our thoughts take us over, rather than being seen by us as arising and passing away in accordance with our choice to follow them or not, to take them up or not.

When we focus on the breath, the breath becomes our anchor in the moment. In meditation it is not that we are with the breath every single second, which would be too difficult. By coming back to the breath again and again, we do not feed distracted thoughts. We loosen the power they have over us by returning to the breath and the whole moment, instead of being caught and defined by one thought. When we are lost in a thought, especially a trivial or mean thought, we can reduce our experience and our identity to that thought, and it might make us act destructively or unskilfully. By coming back to the breath, we let go of that negative thought and increase the power of our wisdom. Do we need to think this? Or could we have a more beneficial, creative and compassionate thought? Nowadays meditation on the breath is used as a medical technique of relaxation, but it also helps people with depression who are caught in their negative repetitive thoughts.

> 'He trains himself, thinking: I will breathe in, conscious of the whole body.' 'He trains himself, thinking: I will breathe out, conscious of the whole body'. 'He trains himself, thinking: I will breathe in, calming the whole bodily process'. 'He trains himself, thinking: I will breathe out, calming the whole bodily process'.
>
> Digha Nikaya, 22

One can focus on the breath in meditation in various ways. Here the Buddha suggests being aware of the in-breath, and through that awareness to be conscious of the whole body. When one uses the breath as an object of meditation, it will help one to calm the mind. At the same time one can focus on the breath and consciously calm the whole body. These instructions of the Buddha have been followed and developed into different methods. One contemporary teacher suggests saying to oneself – 'Breathing in, I calm my body; breathing out, I smile.'

Over time various methods of meditating with the breath were developed from intentionally breathing long breaths or short breaths to counting the breaths. One can even count the breaths in different ways: count each in-breath up to ten and then start again at one, or count each in-breath and out-breath to ten and then count backwards one, for example. When concentrating on the breath; some teachers recommend focusing on the place where the air passes through the nostrils, other teachers suggest observing the rise and fall of the abdomen; and others recommend attending to the whole breath.

MINDFULNESS OF FEELINGS

Dependent on eye and visible forms, eye-consciousness arises; the coincidence of the three is contact; with contact as condition, there arises what is felt as pleasant or as painful or as neither-painful-nor-pleasant. If, on experiencing the contact of pleasant feeling, one does not relish it or welcome or accept it, and if no underlying tendency in one to lust for it any longer underlies it – if, on experiencing the contact of painful feeling, one does not sorrow or lament or heat one's breast, weep or become distraught, and if no underlying tendency in one to resistance to it any longer underlies it – if, on experiencing the contact of neither-painful-nor-pleasant feeling, one understands, as it actually is, the arising, disappearance, gratification, dangerous inadequacy, and escape, in the case of that feeling, and if no underlying tendency in one to ignorance any longer underlies it – then, indeed, that one shall make an end of suffering, by abandoning the underlying tendency to grasp at pleasant feeling, by eliminating the underlying tendency to resist painful feeling, and by abolishing the underlying tendency to ignore neither- painful-nor-pleasant feeling.

Majjhima Nikaya, 148

The Buddha encouraged his disciples to be aware of the basic tonality of their feelings before they become more complex emotions. Our emotional responses are so fast and so intricately connected with stories about the past and the future that it is quite difficult to see how it all begins. For this reason the Buddha suggested being aware of the feeling arising immediately after contact through the senses – eye contact, ear contact, nose contact, tongue contact, body contact, and mind contact. In this meditation one therefore focuses on something one sees or hears, for example, and examines the feeling arising from that contact: is it pleasant, unpleasant or neutral?

Over time, by becoming more aware of these basic feelings or tones one is less caught in a particular feeling, or in the emotion and story it might give rise to. Generally when we experience a pleasant feeling, we do not question it, we accept it as natural. Moreover, we feel that it should continue and the desire to repeat the experience that produced this pleasant feeling is created. The Buddha's way is to be aware of the quality of the feeling without grasping at it. One knows it fully as it happens, but one is not disturbed or destabilised by it.

The Buddha saw two processes at work – how we react to the feelings and how we imagine our future feelings based upon that experience. He understood the danger of being ahead of ourselves. He also recognised that people spend much time living in anticipation – hoping for a pleasant future, anxious about an unpleasant future – instead of creatively engaging with pleasant and unpleasant feelings as they arise and responding accordingly.

The Buddha saw two types of suffering – suffering when we experience painful feelings and suffering when we imagine future painful feelings. The terms he used are: 'to sorrow, lament, beat one's breast, weep or become distraught'. To do this when we encounter a difficult situation is natural, but if we become overwhelmed by these emotional reactions it will not help the situation; on the contrary, it will diminish our possibility to respond skilfully to the situation. Furthermore, if we develop anxiety and fear about future difficult situations, this will be painful and stressful, and it will stop us from developing and cultivating our abilities now when we do not suffer from that specific situation.

The Buddha was conscious of the existence of neutral feeling tones and thought that it was essential to be mindful of them as much as of pleasant feelings or unpleasant feelings. The Buddha felt that in general people ignored neutral feelings and this might make them indifferent. When the feelings are neither pleasant nor unpleasant, we do not feel much, but the Buddha wants us to become even aware of these subtle neutral feelings and to learn to be with them in a different way.

> *Friend Visakha, pleasant feeling is pleasant when it persists and painful when it changes. Painful feeling is painful when it persists and pleasant when it changes. Neither-painful-nor-pleasant feeling is pleasant when there is knowledge [of it] and painful when there is no knowledge [of it].*
>
> *Majjhima Nikaya,* 44

Here it is not the Buddha speaking but a nun, Dhammadina. The answers she gave to a series of questions posed by the lay follower Visakha were approved subsequently by the Buddha and became canonical. She explained at length about people's reactions to feelings and their transience. She pointed out that a pleasant feeling will continue to give us pleasure if it lasts, but if it stops it will be transformed into an unpleasant feeling. A painful feeling will be perceived as painful the longer it persists but will be felt as pleasant when it stops. Recently medical scientists have confirmed this by observing that people can handle short, sharp pains more easily than longer less painful pains; very likely this is because their memory of the first type of cessation was more pleasant than that of the second.

Moreover, Dhammadina suggested that neutral feelings are pleasant when we are aware of them and unpleasant when we are not. If nothing special is happening to us, nothing specifically joyful or painful, we do not feel much. If we were aware of a feeling that is neither pleasant nor unpleasant, it could be deeply restful, because we actually feel calm and tranquil. Because nothing special or extreme is happening, we can rest and just be aware of being alive in this moment and do whatever is required. We might feel like that at work or at home. In a way it might be easier to work in that state as nothing will interfere, we will not be too anxious or too excited, but stable and open in this moment. At home we can use these moments to rest and breathe for a short time – with nothing special to do, nothing special to be.

But if we do not cultivate mindfulness and we feel a neutral feeling it can turn into an unpleasant feeling because of its association with boredom. We will feel that nothing special is happening – nothing specially good, nothing specially bad, and from that we will often generate painful stories about being a boring person, having a boring life, the world being boring, and actually end up in a painful place. Sometimes it seems that we prefer to have painful feelings because they are somewhat exciting and we seem to feel more alive in them than with neutral feelings that we equate with non-existence. This ancient nun was saying that the problem is not with neutral feelings but with our relationship to them and our interpretation of them.

Feeling, perception and consciousness, friend – these states are conjoined, not disjoined, and it is impossible to separate each of these states from the others in order to describe the difference between them; for what one

feels, that one perceives; and what one perceives, that one cognises.
Majjhima Nikaya, 43

When we talk about feeling, perception and consciousness, we analyse and separate them in different categories, which might give the impression that they are distinct and existing separately and independently from each other. Here the Buddha pointed out that feeling, perception and consciousness are intricately connected and linked with each other. When, therefore, we are mindful of feelings, we can become aware of perceptions and thoughts at the same time and vice versa.

When, after doing meditation for a while, we become aware of a feeling, we can look around and see upon which contact that feeling has arisen. It is not a feeling disconnected from the situation in which we find ourselves. If we are caught in some train of thought, we can see how these thoughts are actually evoking certain feelings. For instance, if we are sitting on a bench in a park on a warm day, we might be relatively contented and see someone who looks like a person we know but in fact is not that person. This might trigger a memory of a bad word that person said to us a month ago. If we see that memory as merely an event in that moment just rising and passing away, and that it is not that person, it will not change the feeling of contentment. But if we grasp at that memory and replay it a few times in our head, this will lead us to think of all the bad things that person might have ever done, then of all the bad things other people have done to us, and then we might feel wretched. The Buddha was trying to show us that anything can trigger despondent states in us – it can be a feeling, a perception or a thought. From any of these entrance points we can grasp at something and then it will spread to the whole body and mind organism.

MIND

And how, monks, does a monk abide contemplating mind as mind? Here, a monk knows a lustful mind as lustful, a mind free from lust as free from lust; a hating mind as hating, a mind free from hate as free from hate, a deluded mind as deluded, an undeluded mind as undeluded, a contracted mind as contracted, a distracted mind as distracted....
Digha Nikaya, 22

When one is trying to cultivate mindfulness or presence of mind, one is looking at its content. Basically one is asking: what is going on in my mind? What kind of thoughts am I having? Are my thoughts lustful or unlustful, hateful or kind? Our tendency is to be totally identified with the content of our thoughts. We often have the experience that we are our thoughts, but the Buddha is trying to point out that we have thoughts. We do not constantly think about only one thing; we have all kind of thoughts.

This meditation helps us to see when we are having positive thoughts that might help us to be more wise and compassionate, and when we are having negative thoughts that will lead to suffering and anguish for ourselves and others. Often people think that the aim of meditation is to have no thoughts, but on the contrary the aim of Buddhist meditation is to explore the thoughts that pass through our mind and to notice their types and their qualities, and how they influence our feelings and actions.

From this guidance of the Buddha about being aware of the mind, various types of meditation have been developed. One Burmese meditation exercise, called 'noting', involves paying close attention to every single thought one has and labelling it – planning, dreaming, worrying, and so on. Another method found in the Tibetan tradition is to try to be aware of the space between the thoughts, to see when a thought starts and when it ends, and to notice the in-between state. Another technique found in the Soto Zen Japanese tradition is to be aware of anything that arises without doing anything with it, at the same time neither grasping nor rejecting it.

NON-GRASPING

Try to be like water, Rahula; when people wash away these things with water, for that, water is not ashamed, humiliated or disgusted. Try to be like fire, Rahula; when fire burns these things, for that, fire is not ashamed, humiliated or disgusted.... Try to be like space, Rahula, for by so doing, when agreeable or disagreeable contacts arise, they will not invade your heart and stay there; for space has no standing place of its own.

Majjhima Nikaya, 62

Rahula is the son of the Buddha who followed him to become a monk at an early age. In this quotation the Buddha was giving to his son an indication about the state he wanted his disciples to develop. The Buddha is describing non-grasping through the three metaphors of water, fire and space. Water is used to wash away dirty things, but the water does not take this personally and does not make it a comment on its own worth. The water does what it is asked to do, wash away the dirt, without grasping the dirt or the people who use the water to wash it away. It does not identify with the dirt as 'me' or 'mine'. In the same way, Rahula needed to engage creatively with whatever he encountered without it becoming a judgement about himself, and without his being destabilised by that encounter in reacting negatively to it.

Fire also can be used to burn dirty rubbish and it is not disgusted by that task. The analogy also works with the fact that one is not coloured by what one encounters. The fire burns the rubbish, the rubbish disappears, but the fire does not disappear and remains bright for further use. If we are not caught by our likes or dislikes, if we do not generate stories about how terrible the situation is, we can respond to the situation skilfully and be ready, stable and open for the next situation. The metaphor of space shows us that what the Buddha is concerned with is the way we grasp at what is agreeable and disagreeable. If we are limited to these, they stop us from having a wider perspective. If we create space within, we will be able to have a different relationship with what we encounter.

BALANCE

Similarly, Sona, if energy is applied too forcefully it will lead to restlessness, and if energy is too lax, it will lead to lassitude. Therefore, Sona, keep your energy in balance, penetrate to a balance of the spiritual faculties, and there seize your object.

Anguttara Nikaya, VI, 55

Here the Buddha was talking to a monk called Sona, who was thinking of giving up, because, although he had been practising extremely hard, he felt that he was not becoming free and liberated. The Buddha was a pragmatist and a fine psychologist, and he saw that in the practice as well, one needed to apply the middle way. He realised through his own experiences and those of others that if one tries too hard, is too intent and applies too much energy, then it becomes an obstacle for the practice, as this over-abundant energy would lead one to feel restless and agitated. It is important to apply oneself and make an effort, but within reason.

In Zen, people talk about effortless effort – trying hard, but not too hard – trying in a relaxed but steady manner. The Buddha compared the right attitude to tuning a guitar. If the strings are adjusted too tightly, they will snap. If the strings are too loose, the notes will not sound right. Similarly, if one tries to meditate or practise only half-heartedly, then this will sap the energy one might have and actually lead to disinterest and lassitude. The Buddha encouraged his disciples to develop a balance between trying too hard and too little. For him, it was important to find the middle way when developing mindfulness, investigation, energy, joy, tranquillity, concentration and equanimity.

Chapter Five

Compassion

HAPPINESS FOR SELF AND OTHERS

Seclusion is happiness for one contented,
by whom the Dhamma is learnt, and who has seen,
and friendliness towards the world is happiness
for him that is forbearing with live creatures.
Disinterest in the world is happiness
for him that has surmounted sense desires.
But to be rid of the conceit 'I am' –
that is the greatest happiness

Vinaya Mahavagga, Khandhaka 11

In this poem the Buddha described the different types of happiness one can experience on the Buddhist path. To live on one's own is happiness if one is contented after having studied the Dhamma and understood it. If one understands change, suffering and conditionality, and through meditation develops peace, one will feel confident and alive, and quite happy on one's own.

If someone cares for people and animals, has patience and understanding towards them, it will be easy to feel friendly towards whatever and whoever is alive. One will be able to relate in a positive banner and this will give one a happy feeling. If a person has gone beyond wanting and acquiring, he or she will not identify the valuing of oneself with possessions. This person will appreciate living in a simple manner, using only what he or she needs to survive in a non-acquisitive way. Thus one will not feel constantly attracted and bombarded by outside things coming through the senses. One will be in the world and engaged with it, but not in a stressed and lustful way, and happiness can follow.

But for the Buddha the greatest happiness is to lose the self-centred 'I am'. By this statement the Buddha is not saying that we do not exist but that we do not need to be so self-centred, that the more selfless we are, the happier we will be. Again, the Buddha is not telling us that we must totally forget about ourselves and only think of others; he is trying to point out the danger of self-obsession. If we look into our thoughts, feelings and sensations, we can observe that most of the time they are about 'me' – my desires, my anxieties, my plans, my dreams, my expectations – and even thoughts about family and friends are about me. We can attempt to dissolve this tendency towards self-reference by trying the exercise of replacing 'I' with less personal words. For example, we can try to think 'this person exists, this flow of condition is studying, the five aggregates are walking' and so on. This can help us shift our self-obsession and begin to have a wider sense of self, more conditional and relational rather than static and fixed.

Each person has a tendency to feel that she or he is the centre of the universe, which implies that everything depends on her or him, which is a heavy responsibility. Or that everything should revolve around one, which is extremely solipsistic and not very creative. The Buddha was pointing out that if one loosens one's sense of identity in a positive way, one will be able to connect with, and benefit more from, the world and in turn participate more happily in it.

Monks, for this reason those matters which I have discovered and proclaimed should be thoroughly learnt by you, practised, developed and cultivated, so that this holy life may endure for a long time, that it may be for the benefit and happiness of the multitude, out of compassion for the world, for the benefit and happiness of devas and humans.

Digha Nikaya, 16

The Buddha had two aims. One goal was for his disciples to develop successfully his teachings and his understanding. He did not aspire to become like a god that would just be venerated by the multitude. He wanted his discoveries to be applied and be beneficial to those who followed him. He hoped that his students would achieve what he had achieved. This was the only way that this spiritual path could be continued and sustained over time.

Because he thought that his teachings could be helpful to many people, the Buddha encouraged his disciples to propagate the Dhamma out of compassion. The Buddha found what he had discovered useful and he thought that others could benefit from it too. Again, people at times have thought that Buddhism, being focused on suffering, would lead to sadness and restriction. The Buddha, however, felt that his practice had brought him great joy and happiness, and he wanted others to experience that happiness and joy.

At the time of the Buddha, people in India believed in gods, heavens and hells. The Buddha was reputed to have given special discourses to the gods in the heavens and also to have discussions with *devas* (heavenly beings). One can either believe this as factually true or see it as the cultural manifestation of a medieval mind. Personally I would interpret 'for the benefit of *devas* and humans' as trying to be as inclusive as possible, in order to demonstrate that nobody and nothing is rejected as being incapable of benefiting from the Buddha's teachings.

LOVING-KINDNESS

I maintain bodily acts of loving-kindness towards these venerable ones both openly and privately; I maintain verbal acts of loving-kindness towards them both openly and privately, I maintain mental acts of loving-kindness towards them both openly and privately. I consider: 'Why should I not set aside what I wish to do and do what these venerable ones wish to do?' Then I set aside what I wish to do and do what these venerable ones wish to do. We are different in body, venerable sir, but one in mind.

Majjhima Nikaya, 128

This text refers to the way monks lived together and the atmosphere existing between them. The monk who speaks is stating that he endeavours to cultivate loving-kindness towards his companions. He cultivates loving-kindness, not in an abstract way but in a very concrete manner through kind and loving actions, words and thoughts, in public as well as in private. Sometimes our words might be polite and appear kind, but not our thoughts. Here the monk is showing that we can try to be kind in all ways. Sometimes it might seem more convenient to be kind publicly but not privately; but this monk is trying to be kind at all times, not only when it suits him, and not to impress others or because he feels obligated. He does it because it is his practice and he finds it beneficial for himself, and also for the development of good relationships.

The monk questions why he should act just for his own sake, and finds that he can easily do things for others for their benefit because it brings him joy, happiness and contentment. Although the monks are different, coming from various places and backgrounds, he acts in that selfless way towards them because he sees that they are all intimately connected. They share the air they breathe, the practice they do, and the place they inhabit. They all have the same intention – to follow the teachings of the Buddha and to awaken for the sake of all beings.

It is easy to think that if we consider the wishes of others they will take advantage of us and we will no longer be independent and free. But if we look around, we can see that other people have the same intention as ourselves, to be happy and to be at peace and not to suffer. The example of this Buddhist monk praised by the Buddha can make us reflect on how we relate to others. What is our intention? What are our thoughts, words and actions? What are their results? Do they arise on the basis of the cultivation of loving-kindness? Do they lead to contentment and harmony?

Rahula, develop meditation on loving-kindness; for when you develop meditation on loving-kindness, any ill will be abandoned. Rahula, develop meditation on compassion; for when you develop meditation on compassion, any cruelty will be abandoned. Rahula, develop meditation on appreciative joy; for when you develop meditation on appreciative joy, any discontent will be abandoned. Rahula, develop meditation on equanimity; for when you develop meditation on equanimity, any aversion will be abandoned.

Majjhima Nikaya, 62

Here again the Buddha was giving instructions to his son, Rahula. This passage shows that he encouraged the practice of loving-kindness, compassion, appreciative joy and equanimity for specific reasons. The Buddha was a pragmatist and observed the effects of certain practices on him and others. He found that as one developed loving-kindness, ill-will dissolved; compassion led to the abandonment of cruelty; appreciative joy worked against dissatisfaction; equanimity had an effect on aversion.

The way to practise loving-kindness or good will was to think actively, speak and act in a loving and kind way. One helpful method was to focus on good will in meditation and to recite inwardly and silently a series of short sentences directed towards different types of people. One starts by focusing on oneself, then on people near one, after that on everything alive around one. Then one wishes well to people who are benefactors, then ordinary strangers, then enemies, and finally wishes well to all the sentient beings in the whole world. There is a choice of sentences that could be used:

May I/you/all beings have safety.
May I/you/all beings be happy.
May I/you/all beings be healthy.
May I/you/all beings live with ease.

The idea is to focus on and repeat the sentences in meditation. When one brings oneself or another person to mind, one looks beyond the images one might have of oneself or of that person and reach out to the human being who wants to be happy. The loving-kindness helps one to reflect on the goodness within oneself and others. It allows one to embrace and accept oneself and others, and in turn it will help one to dissolve ill-will.

The sentences for cultivating compassion in meditation are these:

May I/you/all beings be free from pain.
May I/you/all beings be free from sorrow.
May I/you/all beings gain release from all suffering.

Focusing on compassion helps us to be more aware of the suffering we and others experience, thus making us feel and be moved by that pain and so endeavour to relieve it. Bringing specific people to mind makes them more concrete and less abstract. One is more conscious of their actual suffering. It does not mean that one condones their actions if they are destructive, but that one can open one's heart to the people themselves. If we are open to the suffering of the world, cruelty, which involves separation and indifference to the person's plight, can disappear.

The sentences for appreciative joy are these:
May my/your/all beings' good fortune continue.
May my/your/all beings' happiness not diminish.
May I/you/all beings not be deprived of the attainment reached.

When cultivating appreciative joy, we are cultivating our delight in happiness, prosperity and good fortune. It is an antidote to envy and boredom. First, it helps us become conscious of our own good fortune. Secondly, it enables us to rejoice at the happiness of others. We can have a tendency to think that if other people are happy, there will be less happiness for us, but the Buddha sees clearly that happiness is not quantifiable and restricted to a certain measure. All of us can find joys in our lives and if, in addition to this, we rejoice in the happiness of others, this will bring us even more contentment, so reducing discontent and frustrations.

The last quality to cultivate is equanimity, and the phrases associated with it can have a traditional format or a more modern outlook. I shall present examples of both, but first here are the traditional types:

All living beings are owners of their actions.
All living beings have their actions as their refuge.
Whatever action they perform, for good or evil, to that they will fall heir.

Secondly, a more modern version:

May we be undisturbed by the comings and goings of events.
I will care for you but cannot keep you from suffering.
I wish you happiness but cannot make your choices for you.

Thirdly, a shorter modern version:

May we/all beings accept things as they appear.
May we/all beings be balanced.
May we/all beings be at peace.

When we cultivate equanimity, we are trying to avoid the two extremes of grasping or rejecting. We are trying to cultivate an attitude that will help us to encounter the world in a responsible and creative way. For the Buddha, equanimity meditation was especially useful to dissolve the power of aversion and thus of exaggeration.

He abides with a heart endued with abundant, exalted, measureless loving-kindness, unhostile and unafflicted by ill-will, extending to the entire world. He abides with a heart endued with compassion.... He abides with a heart endued with gladness.... He abides with a heart endued with on looking equanimity ... extending to the entire world.

Anguttara Nikaya, III, 65

For the Buddha, the qualities of loving-kindness, compassion, rejoicing and equanimity are not just developed for our own benefit but for the way they will help us to relate to the world in a totally different manner. Sometimes people assume that Buddhist meditation is only about rarefied states of concentration inaccessible to common mortals. Of course, the Buddha enjoyed living in seclusion, but at the same time he was an urban man who was constantly relating to all kinds of people. Various people came to him for succour and he tried to help them skilfully.

Once a lady, whose son had just died, came to him very distraught and asked for his help in reviving her son. The Buddha said that he would help her if she brought him a mustard seed from a house where there had never been a death. She went looking for it everywhere and did not find one. Through that exercise, she reached an understanding of impermanence, as well as compassion for herself and others when confronted with death.

When the Buddha suggested that people investigate change, suffering and selflessness, one of the reasons was that through this investigation, one would experience for oneself change, suffering and selflessness, and the effect of that would be to develop wisdom and compassion together. When we realise the two aspects of impermanence – death and change – compassion arises. When we know that people's lives rest upon a single breath, we know for ourselves the fragility of existence and therefore cannot but have compassion for each being who is so tentatively alive now.

If we act from the knowledge that there is a possibility for transformation and change, we can have a more compassionate attitude towards people and their negative habits. With the help of conditionality we can trust that change is possible and plant seeds to help foster that change, which should be in thoughts, words or actions, even if it might take a long time for these seeds to grow fully and for change to occur. When we see clearly that our existence is totally dependent on forces and energy outside ourselves, we can feel more connection to the world that sustains us and more compassion for all the beings with whom we share this world and this life.

HARMLESSNESS

One morning the Buddha dressed, and taking his bowl and outer robe, he went into Savatthi for alms. Between Jeta's Grove and Savatthi he saw a party of boys ill-treating some fish. He went up to them and asked: 'Boys, are you afraid of pain? Do you dislike pain?'
'Yes, Lord, we are afraid of pain, we dislike pain.'
Knowing the meaning of this, the Buddha then uttered this exclamation:

> *'Whoever does not want to suffer*
> *should do no evil deeds*
> *openly or in secret.*
> *Do evil now, then later,*
> *try though you may to flee it,*
> *yet surely you will suffer.'*

Udana, V, 4

This episode occurred when the Buddha was residing in Jeta's Grove, a park given to him by a generous merchant in Savatthi, capital of Kosala, the kingdom that controlled the part of India that was north of the Ganges. He was on his way to beg alms and he saw boys being cruel to fish. His method was not to remonstrate with them directly but to encourage them to reflect on pain and suffering – their own and that of others.

To help people give rise to compassion, the Buddha made them aware of the equality of life. Each life is equal in happiness and offering. When I suffer, it is painful and I am alone. When someone else suffers, in the same way it is painful for him or her, and he or she is also alone. The Buddha is trying to enable people to develop empathy by showing the commonality of human existence. By losing self-identification and developing other-identification, one could be more easily touched and connected to the plight of others, instead of feeling separate and indifferent.

This poem also shows the idea of causality and conditionality as connected to compassion. If we cause suffering to others, we are likely to experience suffering also later on. This could be interpreted in several ways. One is through the notion of karma, the idea that we will harvest what we plant. If we cause suffering intentionally, we put some energy in motion that will come back to us in the future. Another view could be that in the same way that we disregard the suffering of others, some people will disregard the suffering they cause us. If we can do this to another, someone else can do it to us. The idea, therefore, is that if we cultivate compassion, we will receive compassion too in the future. But the most important point is that we should not add to the pain and suffering of the world. One point the Buddha made is that destructive actions, whether done out in the open or in secret, will have the same result. It is not the fact that people see you doing the actions that matters but the fact that you had the intention to cause pain and carried it out.

> *If a grudge arises towards any person, then one should cultivate loving-kindness towards him ... or compassion ... or equanimity. In that way one can remove the grudge towards that person.*
>
> Anguttara Nikaya, V, 161

When there are any bad feelings towards someone, we have a tendency to become obsessed by them and fixated on any bad behaviour, however insignificant, that they might show. If, instead, we realised that they do not always do negative things and we tried to remember some of the positive things they might have done for us or for others, this might help to dissolve our grudges.

If we feel resentment towards someone for some slight done to us, our resentment will not change the situation in any way and it is we who suffer from the resentment, not the other person. But if we have compassion for our own suffering, we will be able to let go of the resentment that is tormenting us. Moreover, if we see that the person did not hurt us intentionally but because they were suffering themselves, it might help us to have more understanding and to find a more creative and wise way to resolve the situation.

When we bear some grievance about some situation because we feel it is unfair, if we bring equanimity to mind, it might remind us that we cannot expect the world and every situation to be fair. This would enable us to dissolve our rancour, to come back to a more stable and open posture, and see what we could do actively to change the conditions so that the situation could be more balanced and relaxed.

> *There are, monks, successes in living caused by wholesome volition, issuing in happiness, resulting in happiness.... There is the person who abstains from the destruction of life; with the rod and weapon laid*

aside, he is conscientious and kindly, and dwells compassionate towards
all living beings....

Anguttara Nikaya, X, 206

Here again, the Buddha is pointing out that happiness comes from a compassionate attitude and is dependent on our intention. If our intention is to be harmless, not to cause any loss of life, not to destroy any living beings, then contentment will follow. This will involve being conscious of our actions and their results, being kind and compassionate towards all beings. The Buddha's monks and nuns were reputed for their harmlessness – they would not even destroy blades of grass.

The precepts of the monastics prevent them from being farmers as this profession involves the destruction of lives, be it that of insects, animals or plants. This is why the Buddha wanted his monks and nuns to beg for their food. He realised that farming had to exist for people to survive, but that the monks and nuns could have simple lives, eating only one meal a day and benefiting from the surplus food created by people. For this reason the monastic chants at meal times mention the hardships people, animals and plants suffered for the food the monks and nuns eat, and so not even a grain of rice should be wasted.

He has no ill-will in his heart. He has pure thoughts and intentions,
such as these: 'May these beings be free from enmity, free from anxiety!
May they be untroubled and live happily!'

Anguttara Nikaya, X, 206

When one is practising loving-kindness or compassion meditation, one is not trying to produce specific feelings in the heart but to cultivate a certain attitude of mind, so that over time our whole being will be orientated in the direction of loving-kindness and compassion. The Buddha recognised that people have an innate capacity for loving-kindness and compassion. The meditations he suggested are not to create something out of nothing, but to deepen and hone these innate feelings, thoughts and intentions that are within human beings already. His methods were to make them arise and be manifested in a more universal way.

It is easy to be loving, kind and compassionate towards people we like, and who are friendly towards us. It is much harder to have these thoughts and intentions towards people we find difficult or that we do not like. In the meditation we start by focusing on ourselves, because we need to feel compassion for ourselves if we want to manifest this more universal type of compassion towards all beings. As people can sometimes be severe judges of themselves, the Buddha is saying that anyone is worthy to receive compassion, ourselves included.

If we focus first on people we like, whose company we enjoy, and who are supportive, it helps us to move more easily in that stream and make it easier to send compassionate thoughts and wishes to them. We focus on strangers or people we might feel indifferent to in order to connect to their lives and to their suffering, to see that they too have a history, they too are human beings who aspire to happiness. We have to be careful when we focus in meditation on people with whom we have difficulties. It is essential not to get lost and caught up in why we dislike them. We have to envisage them as human beings who suffer and to wish them well. The idea is not for us to recall the differences we have with them but for us to try to open our heart, thoughts and intentions to their humanity and their pains. The Buddha is trying to make people develop a loving-kindness and a compassion that would permeate their whole being and that would help them think, speak and act in a compassionate way in all aspects of their lives.

Chapter Six

Ethics

RESPONSIBILITY

Beings are owners of their actions, heirs of their actions; they originate from their actions, are bound to their actions, have their actions as their refuge. It is action that distinguishes beings as inferior and superior.

Majjhima Nikaya, 135

'Action', in this instance, is the translation of the word karma. In the popular imagination karma seems to be equated with destiny or fate. But karma just means action, in Buddhist terms to act out of an intention conditioned by external and internal conditions, which in turn will have a certain result and will leave a certain imprint. In the Buddha's time this was seen within the concept of rebirth. Thus one was said to be reborn in accordance with one's actions, the intentions that motivated them, the way they were accomplished, and the result that ensued. Professor H.W. Schumann called it 'ethical conditionalism'. He explained it in this way: 'Rebirth in good or bad circumstances is not a reward or punishment for good and bad deeds but their natural consequences.'

One has to be careful that although in this vision the person conditions the rebirth, the two people are not identical. It is not the same person who is reborn. Moreover, it does not mean that everything that we experience in this life is due to past actions. The Buddha saw karmic consequences as one of eight causes – troubles with the three bodily humours, separate and together (phlegm, bile and wind), seasonal change, improper care, exertion, and ripening of former actions – or one of five conditions, meteorological, biological, physical, psychological and karmic. In terms of ordinary people, ethical actions would lead to better rebirth. In terms of walking actively on the noble eightfold path, it would lead to nirvana. In both cases the cultivation of ethical actions would help one to dissolve egoism. The arahants were said to act ethically naturally, so it would not even occur to them to behave unethically.

The Buddha saw ethics as the basis for spiritual progress. It is for this reason that he regarded ethics as more important than metaphysics. The Buddha moved the focus of the spiritual search away from what the world was to how one should behave. In the Upanishads one finds the notion of an absolute self, in Buddhism the notion of moral agency. The Buddha believed that there is possibility of human choice and freedom of action, but that actions become true actions only if they are conscious, thought about and intentional.

Professor R.F. Gombrich thinks that in the Upanishads the aim 'to realise the self as only reality is to realise what has always been the case: change and movement were an illusion. In the Buddha's world one has to make things happen.' In Brahminism one purified oneself and thus removed evil and pollution through the act of washing; in Buddhism purification was equated with spiritual progress, which was conditioned by cultivating ethics. So one sees a movement from ethics based on certain ritual actions of purification to ethics based on psychological processes. Salvation, therefore, did not depend on one's caste, one's birth and one's superior rituals, but on how one lived. For the Brahmin, to lead a good life meant performing the right sacrifice and avoiding pollution, which in turn help him or her towards a better rebirth. For the Buddha, it was purely an ethical matter of thoughts, words and deeds. It did not depend on special sacrifices and rituals.

This is why, in the first stage of awakening, the belief in rites and rituals disappears. If the goodness of the person does not depend on rites and rituals, it is better to let that belief go and instead concentrate on one's actions and motivations, which is what for the Buddha would make a difference in terms of dissolving greed, hatred and ignorance.

FIVE PRECEPTS

When a lay follower possesses five things, he lives with confidence in his house, and he will find himself in heaven as sure as if he had been carried there. What are the five? He abstains from killing breathing things, from taking what is not given, from misconduct in sensual desires, from speaking falsehood, and from indulging in liquor, wine, and fermented brews.

Anguttara Nikaya, V, 173

For the Buddha, behaving ethically had two advantages: the first one had to do with this life and the other with a future life. Over the centuries ethics was more and more associated with effects in a future life. But the Buddha's teachings showed a clear concern about the effects in this life. He suggested that to behave ethically would help one to live with confidence in one's home. If one does not kill, does not steal, does not behave in an improper manner sexually, does not lie and does not become drunk, one is not causing suffering to oneself or to others and as such can feel at peace with oneself and with the world and be confident in one's own life and actions.

The Buddha based his ethics on the two concepts of moral shame (*hiri*) and moral dread (*ottapa*). The former describes the inner shame one would feel about acting unethically. Our own self-respect would stop us from killing or stealing, for example. It would not feel right to act in such a way. It is like a personal code of honour. The second concept, moral dread, is more concerned with the results of negative actions in the external world. One would be conscious of three different consequences: blame and punishment from others, negative karmic consequences, and acting unethically would create obstacles to liberation from suffering and so to the attainment of awakening.

For the Buddha, one abstains not just from killing people, but also from killing anything that breathes. He is conscious of the value of life in its entirety. In his time there were animal sacrifices and immediately he suggested to his followers that they should not engage in such actions, but if they wanted to sacrifice anything in ceremonies, they should instead offer flowers, incense or clarified butter. The injunction about not stealing is expressed as not taking what is not given, and so invites us to become more conscious about our relationship with property and more specifically the property of others. We might think that we are not really stealing if we take something that belongs to someone else but that he or she is not using. For the Buddha, as long as something is not given directly then it is an infraction, because it is taking the property of another for one's own benefit without their authorisation, which then can lead to conflict or misunderstanding later on.

About misconduct in sensual desires the Buddha stated: 'He avoids unlawful sexual intercourse, abstains from it. He has no intercourse with girls who are still under the protection of father or mother, brother, sister or relatives, nor with married women, nor female convicts, nor, lastly, with betrothed girls.' In modern times, misconduct in sensual desires means engaging in sexual acts with an inappropriate person in a harmful way. This would include adultery, child molestation, incest, rape, sexual abuse in any form, and sexual harassment. The Buddha was pointing out that indulging sexual desires without moderation would not help one on the eightfold path. Moreover, if one were to disregard the feelings of others or act sexually in a way involving violence, manipulation or deceit, this would be harmful.

I will talk more at length later about 'not speaking falsehood' as the Buddha put great emphasis on right speech throughout his life. He was also aware of the damage caused by intoxication with alcohol. Since the Buddha praised clarity of mind above all, drunkenness would have the opposite effect. Again, this was in line with his recommendations to be aware of conditions, actions and their consequences. The difficulty was not with the substance itself but with the effect alcohol had on people once it was ingested; as it could lead to foolish acts and even more dangerously to violence and harm. In the *Sigalovada Sutta* the Buddha shows his pragmatism and awareness of human behaviour when he describes the six negative consequences of indulging in intoxicants – loss of wealth, increase in quarrels, susceptibility to disease earning an evil reputation, shameless exposure of the body, and weakening of the intellect. In the two thousand five hundred years since the time of the Buddha, the effects of alcohol on human beings do not seem to have changed much.

NON-AGGRESSION

Here, monks, a noble disciple gives up the destruction of life and abstains from it. By abstaining from the destruction of life, the noble disciple gives

to immeasurable beings freedom from fear, freedom from hostility and
freedom from oppression. By giving to immeasurable beings freedom
from fear, hostility and oppression, he himself will enjoy immeasurable
freedom from fear, hostility and oppression.

Anguttara Nikaya, VIII, 39

Buddhist ethics is based not so much on the notion of the right things
to do in terms of ethnic, social or cultural mores, but on the notion of
suffering and non-harming. Here the Buddha looks at the consequences
of non-harming foremost in terms of the well-being of others, but also of
one's own well-being. If we restrain our actions and refrain from destroying
lives in any way, other people and beings will immediately benefit from our
harmlessness as they will not have to fear us, nor feel oppressed by us. At
the same time, if we are not hostile to anyone we can also feel freedom
from fear as we do not provoke other people's aggression.

And how, monks, does a person live both for his own good and for the
good of others? He himself practises for the removal of lust, hatred and
delusion, and also encourages others to do so.... He himself practises
abstention from killing and so forth, and also encourages others in such
restraint.

Anguttara Nikaya, IV, 96, 99

The Buddhist moral precepts are not commandments but recommendations
for a wholesome way of life. The Buddha wants each disciple to do what is
best for him or her and also what is best for other people. Buddhist ethics
are not an end in themselves, as the precepts are not sacred in themselves.
One cultivates morality in order to help dissolve greed, hatred and delusion.
The Buddha is also concerned that individual changes might be limited
to one person when ethics could benefit the whole society. Therefore he
thought that one should also try to do one's best to encourage others to
be harmless. He did not mean, however, that one should force others as
then they might not listen, but the best way to encourage others was to
set an example in practical terms and live harmlessly.

The Buddha also put great emphasis on good friendship. He repeatedly
told how helpful it could be to have good friends in one's life and on
the eightfold path. In the *Sigalovada Sutta* he defines a warm-hearted friend
as one who gives good counsel in four ways. The Buddha sees a good

friend as restraining one from doing evil, encouraging one to do good, informing one of what is unknown to oneself, and pointing out the path to heaven.

RIGHT LIVELIHOOD

These five trades, O monks, should not be taken up by a lay follower: trading with weapons, trading in living beings, trading in meat, trading in intoxicants, trading in poison.

Anguttara Nikaya, V, 177

Here the Buddha talks about right livelihood for lay people, which is one part of the eightfold path. Basically he defines right livelihood as earning one's living from an occupation that will not cause harm in any way. The first livelihood to avoid, of course, is making and selling weapons or any implements that could be used to hurt people or animals. In the Buddha's time slavery existed, and so he forbade his followers to buy or sell slaves. Similarly, since buying and selling meat involved killing animals, this was not recommended. Since he saw clearly the dangers of drinking and taking drugs, he did not want his disciples to be involved with trading in intoxicants. Finally, since poisons were harmful, he did not recommend the making and selling of them.

At the same time, the Buddha was not against commerce or any other useful occupation. He was very conscious that lay people needed to earn money in order to live. He encouraged his followers to create wealth and to take good care of it. For the Buddha, a balanced livelihood involved knowing one's income and expenses, being neither extravagant nor miserly, so that one's income would be able to cover one's expenses. Again, the Buddha suggested the middle way and the need to avoid living beyond one's means. In the *Vyaggapajja Sutta* he sets the four sources of increasing one's wealth as abstinence from drunkenness, non-indulgence in gambling, friendship, and intimacy with the good. In the *Mahamangala Sutta* he sees the highest protection for a lay person as being consistency in work, supporting one's parents, wife, children and relations, and being generous in general.

There are five ways in which a master should minister to his servants and workpeople...: by arranging their work according to their strength, by supplying them with food and wages, by looking after them when they are ill, by sharing special delicacies with them, and by letting them off work at the right time.

Digha Nikaya, 31

This passage comes from the *Sigalovada Sutta* (also known as the *Sigalaka Sutta*), a discourse the Buddha gave to Sigala, a young man who lived in Rajgir and who, following his dying father's advice, went to worship daily the six directions with wet hair and wet clothes. When the Buddha saw him doing this he suggested that there was a different way to worship the six directions which could be much more beneficial to Sigala. Then the Buddha gave this long discourse, which became later known as the lay person codes of discipline, in which he gave practical advice on how to live a mindful and harmless life. Here he kept the same name – worshipping the six directions – and transformed a Brahminical ritual into a precise series of recommendations of an ethical nature.

The Buddha urged Sigala to abandon four kinds of negative actions, to let go of evil due to four causes, not to fall into the six ways of wasting one's substance. The four negative actions are as mentioned above: killing, stealing, sexual misconduct and lying. The four causes are attachment, ill-will, folly, and fear. The six ways of wasting one's substance are addiction to alcohol and drugs, haunting the streets late at night, attending fairs, addiction to gambling, keeping bad company, and laziness. The Buddha also recommends to Sigala to protect the six directions in the guise of mother and father in the east, teachers in the south, wife and children in the west, friends and companions in the north, servants, workers and helpers in the nadir, and ascetics and Brahmins in the zenith. He finished his discourse by describing five ways in which people in each category can take care of each other – parents and children, teachers and disciples, wife and husband, self and friends, master and servants, self and ascetics.

This passage concerns the relationship between master and servants. The Buddha, mindful of working conditions, is quite modern in his outlook by recommending that work should be suited to the strength of the servant. The supply of food and wages will necessarily make a worker happier and ensure a more comfortable relationship. By suggesting that the master should take care of the servant when he or she was ill, foremost in the Buddha's mind is suffering and the alleviation of suffering and the development of a human and reasonable relationship beyond the idea of strict performance and profit. He even suggested the sharing of special food with the workers as a treat, as a way to make them feel appreciated and valued. The fact that he recommended precise finishing times for work and suggested giving workers time off to rest and recuperate seems to imply that when he was in Sakya with his father he noticed what was helpful and not helpful in terms of the master-servant relationship.

In return, he suggested that the servants and workpeople should get up earlier than the master and retire later than their master, only take what was given to them, and behave properly so as not to besmirch their master's reputation. The Buddha again seemed to be concerned with equilibrium and reciprocity, kindness and respect. He saw these values as important as a way to develop positive and beneficial relationship at all kinds of levels.

VIRTUE

> It is by living with a person that his virtue is to be known, great king, and then only after a long time, not after a short period; and only by considering it, not without consideration; and only by one who is wise, not by a fool. It is by associating with a person that his purity is to be known.... It is in adversity that a person's fortitude is to be known.... It is by discussion with a person that his wisdom is to be known, great king, and then only after a long time, not after a short period; and only by considering it, not without consideration; and only by one who is wise, not by a fool.
>
> Udana,VI, 2

This passage refers to an occasion when the Buddha met King Pasenadi of Kosala in the street. The King pointed out to the Buddha a group of mendicants with all the attributes that mendicants were supposed to have and he asked the Buddha if he thought that they were awakened. The Buddha replied in the words just cited. After he had said this, King Pasenadi told him that this was very true, since these mendicants were no mendicants at all, but his spies, and as soon as they had made their reports, each of them gave up all the mendicant's attributes and lived the indulgent life of a lay person.

Nowadays, too, people wonder if this or that teacher, or religious, or spiritual person, is enlightened or not. Here the Buddha is pointing out that it is difficult to know someone else. Sometimes on the religious or spiritual path it is easy to glorify someone. One can be impressed by the charisma of a powerful person. One can also be attracted by people's breadth of knowledge. One can be seduced by the wonderful words a skilful orator can use; moreover, one can be influenced by her monastic or ascetic clothes, or his humble demeanour. But this was not what the Buddha thought will help one to know the true value of the person. For him, the essential qualities were virtue, purity, fortitude and understanding.

The Buddha gave a precise way to know the worth of someone, which is not a mental test but a living test, and this test is not only for the other person but for oneself as well. So in order to know someone's virtue, we need to live close to that person for a long period of time. Then, on our side of the observation, we need to be attentive to the other person's actions and also to have a certain understanding so that we are not easily deluded. By virtue, the Buddha is referring to the keeping of the precepts and behaving in an ethical way. First, is the person consistent in their actions or not? Do they engage in unwholesome actions or not? Does he or she keep to their principles or just follow their desires regardless of the consequences?

The second thing to observe is purity. For the Buddha, purity refers to the way one behaves towards others. Is one two-faced or not? Does one relate in the same way to another person irrespective of who it is that one encounters? Or is one pleasant when with someone, but nasty about them when discussing that person with others? Does one say the same thing when with one person, several persons or a whole group of people? To put it another way, is one consistent in dealings with other people? In order to know this, one would have to associate for a while with a person to be able to see that person in all manner of settings.

The Buddha admired and encouraged fortitude, patience and endurance when faced with difficulties. It is easy to be calm and to show equanimity when there are no difficulties. But how does one react when confronted by personal loss, whether it be material, in relationships or in terms of status? The Buddha was suggesting that truly to know the quality of a person one would have to see them in times of adversity. Nowadays teachers are put on a pedestal and often everything is done for them. It would be hard to see how they deal with difficulties. It is easy to look profound and awakened on a throne, but how would one behave on the road in the middle of the night in the rain with a punctured tyre?

How does one know if someone is wise or not? This is not easy. The criterion for the Buddha is to discuss many different subjects with the person at great length, in many different ways, over a long period of time. But in this case one would also need to have a certain understanding and be able to think for oneself.

RIGHT SPEECH

He does not in full awareness speak falsehood for his own ends or for another's ends or for some petty worldly end. Abandoning malicious speech, he abstains from malicious speech; he does not repeat elsewhere what he has heard here in order to divide [those people] from these, nor does he repeat to these people what he has heard elsewhere in order to divide [these people] from those; thus he is one who reunites those who are divided, a promoter of friendships, who enjoys concord, rejoices in concord, delights in concord, a speaker of words that promote concord. Abandoning harsh speech, he abstains from harsh speech; he speaks such words as are gentle, pleasing to the ear and lovable, as go to the heart, are courteous, desired by many and agreeable to many. Abandoning gossip, he abstains from gossip; he speaks, at the right time, what is factual and good, about the Dhamma and the Discipline; at the right time he speaks words worth recording, reasonable, moderate and beneficial.

Majjhima Nikaya, 41

Here the Buddha is talking about right speech, its conditions and its consequences. First, one does not lie intentionally for one's own benefit or for someone else's benefit, or for some light material reason. The principal point to notice concerns intention. We could lie by accident or because we are ill-informed, or out of absent-mindedness. We might have forgotten that we know something that we say we do not know.

What the Buddha is discouraging is lying intentionally for a self-serving purpose. Or – and again here the Buddha is looking at multiple causes – we could lie on behalf of someone else. Or we could lie just for fun or for petty reasons, and here the problem is that we might get used to it and then start to lie about bigger and more important things. We might also lie in order not to hurt someone else's feelings, but later that person might reproach us for it. It could have been vital information they feel they needed to know at that time. Not to tell lies is also asking us to reflect on the way we speak and the effects our words have on others. Can we learn to say things more creatively, wisely and kindly?

At times would it be better to say nothing or just 'no comment'? To say something sometimes creates difficulties and it could be better to remain silent. Then we would have to cultivate wise and compassionate silence because certain silences can be felt as more painful than the most cutting words. So we might need to be as aware of the effects of our words as of our silences.

The Buddha's main concerns are about harmony and unity. In that respect, how we speak to others about other people is essential. Do we spread calumny in such a way that we create dissensions between people? People like to talk about other people when they are not present, and then might go and repeat what was heard to the person concerned with sometimes painful results. But isn't it selfish to indulge in such action? Aren't harmony and good relationships more important? It is generally dangerous to answer the question: 'What do(es) he/she/they think of me?' It is a minefield. If it is positive feedback, it might be fine, but even then according to the way we are going to present the information we might or might not foster harmony. Sometimes we might not report properly what was being said or we might use such different words that we will give the whole story a different meaning or the possibility of a different interpretation.

The Buddha is also suggesting that we refrain from harsh or abusive speech. What is interesting is that the abuse can have many different forms. It can be in the words we are using, which might be denigrating, coarse, disrespectful or hurtful. Or it could be the way the words are pronounced in a disdainful or aggressive manner. It could also be our body language when we say certain words without looking at the person directly, offhandedly or dismissively. How can we speak kind words that are pleasing to the ear, lovable, go to the heart, and that are also courteous? It is an important practice. In modern life things go so much faster that sometimes we would like speech to be fast too, but quick words can be dangerous and confusing. It can be helpful to speak more slowly, to take our time to think, to reflect on what would be the best way to express something, so that the other person can really hear what we are saying and understand that it comes from a non-threatening position.

It is difficult to avoid gossiping, because generally we love to gossip, to pass on funny stories, to share the latest weird actions of someone; we enjoy saying negative things about a common enemy. We want to know the latest gossip so we can pass it on before anyone else. But if we reflect on the way we gossip, we might find that it is quite empty and not so helpful. It is important, of course, to be able to take part in small talk as it helps to soften social intercourse. It is not necessary to be incredibly profound and deep at all times, which could be quite exhausting. But can our small talk be appropriate, factual, and connected to the good as the Buddha encourages us to do? Can it uplift us? Can it be light and joyful? Can it be kind and caring?

Chapter Seven

Peace

GOOD GOVERNANCE

This thought arose in his mind while he was alone on retreat: 'Is it possible to govern without killing and ordering execution, without confiscating and sequestrating, without sorrowing and inflicting sorrow, in other words righteously?'

Samyutta Nikaya, IV, 20

This passage shows us that the Buddha's concerns extended widely. He was not only focused on the well-being of his community and his followers but was also interested in how governing could be carried out in a harmless and peaceful way. He was not thinking in terms of doing so himself but of how a king or a group of people such as the Sakyans could govern in a better way. Most of his contact had been with the governing method of King Bimbisara in the Magadha kingdom, of King Pasenadi of the Kosala kingdom, and the republic of the Licchavis, which was part of the Vajjian confederacy.

When he reflected in this way he was in Kosala and he was wondering if it was possible to govern in a peaceful manner. He was aware that in all the kingdoms that he knew, the state carried out executions, confiscation and sequestration. King Bimbisara had been a spiritual and benevolent king, but after thirty years of reign he had been killed by his son, who had wanted his power. The Vajjian confederacy had an interesting method of governing, which was shared more widely. It could work as long as the members of the confederacy governed in harmony, but when they began to quarrel, the son of Bimbisara took advantage of their disharmony to vanquish them. Moreover, the son of King Pasenadi destroyed the Buddha's country of birth. This historical instance seems to show us that governing justly without causing any harm is not easily achieved even with a Buddha present.

Buddhist peace was achieved and just government occurred two hundred years later with King Ashoka (304 BCE–232 BCE) of the Maurya dynasty. But even he started out as a warrior king. Through bloody battles he conquered all of Northern India and territories as far south as Mysore. His capital was in Magadha. He converted to Buddhism after the battle of Kalinga. He was so appalled by that massacre that he decided to abandon further conquest and dedicated himself to building a peaceful nation. He had many monuments erected at the important Buddhist pilgrimage sites. These monuments were rediscovered in the nineteenth century and they showed Ashoka promulgating peace and tolerance through various edicts carved on rocks and pillars. These edicts presented various reforms, policies and spiritual advice to his subjects.

NON-HATRED

'He abused me, he struck me,
he defeated me, he robbed me' –
in those who harbour thoughts like these
hatred will never be allayed.

For in this world hatred is never
allayed by further acts of hate.
It is allayed by non-hatred:
that is the fixed and ageless law.

Those others do not recognise
that here we should restrain ourselves.
But those wise ones who realise this
at once end all their enmity.

Majjhima Nikaya, 128

Here the Buddha is expressing an important Buddhist principle that revenge does not help as it becomes a vicious cycle. If someone abuses us and we abuse them in return, then they will abuse us again in turn, and generally the conflict will escalate. If someone beats us and we start to fight with them, unless we are much stronger we will both be seriously hurt. If someone takes advantage of us and we try to do the same, then it might continue endlessly until one or other of us does not have the energy to continue. If someone robs us and we try to steal from them too, this might continue in the same vein, but at the strong risk of escalation and more danger.

What are the Buddha's solutions to conflict? They are amity, restraint and awareness. In conflict the Buddha taught his disciples to consider the conditions before, during and after the conflict. In many passages the Buddha recommended to his disciples to be prudent and in general not to go to dangerous places where one is likely to be done harm. One of his suggestions is not to go out late at night as one might encounter trouble. Another recommendation is to avoid drink, so as not to become confused and querulous. Another piece of advice is to try not to be quarrelsome and irritable. The first point, therefore, is to try to create conditions where people are less likely to abuse or steal from us.

It is true, however, that people and circumstances are unpredictable, so we can find ourselves in a dangerous situation not of our own making. The Buddha is saying that what is going to help us in these situations is to try to remain calm and stable, and instead of reacting automatically in kind or with negativity, to try to find a more creative way to deal with the situation. And then friendliness, restraint and awareness would be useful. What is our body language? How do we express ourselves? Are we preparing a riposte even before anything has happened? If we project aggression, we are more likely to be subjected to it in return. If we project friendliness, often it is what we will also experience in return.

Restraint can often have a negative connotation in our modern liberated world. But restraint means to have respect for oneself and for others, and also to be careful about giving full-blown expression to our emotional, mental and physical habits too quickly. Can we control ourselves a little and learn to wait, reconsider and creatively engage with a situation, instead of reacting automatically? Sometimes we accuse someone of having taken something when actually we might have misplaced it. And if someone steals from us, of course it is unpleasant, but cultivating hate will not help us to retrieve our goods.

If someone tries to hit or harm us, the Buddha is not telling us to be passive but to be aware. When this happens we are either surprised or fearful, which can often paralyse us and leave us defenceless. Mindful awareness would help us to see it coming and prepare us to take a stance, to flee or to call for help. Mindful awareness might also help us to defuse the situation.

ANGULIMALA

Angulimala, I have stopped forever,
I abstain from violence towards living beings;
but you have no restraint towards things that live:
this is why I have stopped and you have not.

Majjhima Nikaya, 86

This passage is taken from the *Angulimala Sutta.* In this text, there is this wonderful image of the Buddha walking at a normal pace and a murderous pursuer who wanted to kill him but was unable to catch up with him however fast he ran. So the murderer, Angulimala, exclaimed to the Buddha that he should stop. Then the Buddha turned towards him and told him that he, the Buddha, had already stopped any harm towards any beings but Angulimala had not, and that this was why the murderer could not catch him. This episode happened in the twentieth year of the Buddha's teachings. For a while Angulimala had been murdering people in a region of Kosala. His name meant 'finger garland' as he was in the habit of cutting a finger from each person he had killed and threading it onto a necklace he wore around his neck.

The Buddha had decided to walk along the road where Angulimala was known to commit his deadly deeds, notwithstanding people's advice not to go there because it was too dangerous. Upon seeing the Buddha, Angulimala decided to kill him but could not reach him. He was struck by the Buddha's words to stop all violence and become peaceful. He did just that, there and then, and following the Buddha's advice became ordained. He became a diligent and serious monk and attained the supreme Buddhist goal, arahant-ship. In modern times Angulimala is a symbol of the possibility of transformation in the Buddhist tradition, even from extremely serious offences. People who bring the teachings of the Buddha into jails and teach meditation to help prisoners often use the example of Angulimala's life and redemption.

Let my enemies hear discourse on the Dhamma,
let them be devoted to the Buddha's teaching,
let my enemies wait on those good people
who lead others to accept the Dhamma.

Let my enemies give ear from time to time
and hear the Dhamma of those who preach forbearance,
of those who speak as well in praise of kindness,
and let them follow up that Dhamma with kind deeds.

Majjhima Nikaya, 86

This passage is also in the *Angulimala Sutta*, though it is not pronounced by the Buddha but by Angulimala when returning from alms-begging one day. Often when he went begging for food people would assault him, throwing mud and different projectiles, as they had not forgotten nor forgiven him his previous murderous deeds. On that occasion the Buddha told him that he had to bear with it as he was experiencing the fruit of his previous actions. But this did not discourage Angulimala as the meditation practice had helped him to develop equanimity.

Angulimala then reflected on the changes that had occurred in him, that he had gone from mindlessness to wisdom, from murderous actions to skilful actions, and that his devotion to the Buddha and his teachings had been illuminating. As a result, he hoped that his enemies too could benefit from hearing the Dhamma. Moreover, he hoped that people who wished him harm could listen to spiritual guides who extol patience and endurance, but also that they would be able to hear from teachers who celebrated kindness and who practised it themselves.

Angulimala seemed to have been moved and transformed by the way the Buddha treated him. In their first encounter the Buddha not only showed no fear of him but looked beyond Angulimala's cruel actions to the man who could be transformed. Although up to that point Angulimala had been violent, the Buddha treated him as someone who could change and become a peaceful and harmless person. Thereafter Angulimala was struck by the kindly way the Buddha treated him, and very likely this was the same way the Buddha treated anyone. Angulimala could see that there was no difference between the words of the Buddha and his actions.

EQUANIMITY

Uncontrolled people pierce one with words
as they pierce a battle-elephant with arrows.
On hearing harsh words being uttered to him
a bhikkhu should endure them without hate.

Udana, IV, 8

In this passage there is again the strong notion of peacefulness, equanimity and non-retaliation. The episode from which it comes is interesting. The Buddha was staying near Savatthi in the Jeta Wood and because he and his followers were well respected, they were reciving much praise and many offerings. Some other wanderers who were less appreciated and in consequence did not receive as much in the way of homage and offerings were dismayed by the situation and decided to do something about it.

They arranged for a female wanderer to be seen visiting Jeta Wood, after which they killed her and buried her there. Then they publicly accused the Buddha and his followers of having committed murder. As a result, whenever the Buddhist monastics went to beg for alms in Savatthi they were rebuked and shouted at, which distressed them. They therefore went to the Buddha and asked for advice. The Buddha told them that it would pass in seven days, so they should not worry about it, but what they could do was to recite a verse, which would proclaim their innocence. They then did what he suggested, which changed people's minds and, as he foresaw, people stop reviling them after seven days.

The Buddha pointed out two things to his followers: first that things would change, second that they could proclaim their innocence in a peaceful manner. He did not imply that the harsh words they received were not painful. However unpleasant the abuse was, the monastics should not react, and they needed to remain equanimous and dignified. At the same time, he did not suggest that they remain passively undisturbed. There were grounds for the abusive words, so they needed to show in a skilful way that they were not guilty of the murder.

The first two lines of the four-line verse to be recited, whenever someone rebuked them, were: 'The false accuser goes to hell, and also one who denies the deed he did'. This enabled the people of the town to question what they had falsely heard. Since up to that point the Buddha and his followers had been harmless, the people realised that they could not have changed so dramatically and so they realised that the accusation had been false. The fact that the woman wanderer was found murdered in the Jeta Wood did not mean that they were the culprits, even though they lived in the Jeta Wood. By not retaliating and remaining peaceful, the Buddha and his followers did not aggravate the hatred surrounding them and by engaging creatively with the situation were able to transform it positively.

NON-VIOLENCE

All tremble at violence, all fear death, putting oneself in the place of another, one should not kill nor cause another to kill.

Dhammapada

The Buddha was a fervent advocate of non-violence. He constantly counselled people to be harmless. He tried whenever he could to resolve disputes. The most famous episode could be called the Rohini incident. Rohini was the name of a river that flowed between two Sakya clans, the Gotamas and the Koliyas. A dam had been erected to benefit people on both sides of the river. When a drought occurred, however, farmers on both sides of the river started to quarrel about the use of the scarce water remaining in the river. The conflict reached such a pitch that the Gotamas and the Kolyans started to engage in a battle. When the Buddha realised what was happening, he hastened to help them to resolve their dispute. He convinced them that killing each other over water would spill much blood and create a great deal of suffering. He did so in such a skilful way that all enmity ceased and peace was re-established.

Chapter Eight

Transmission

SELF-RELIANCE

But Gotami, when you know of certain things – 'These things lead to dispassion, not to passion; to detachment, not to bondage; to diminution, not to accumulation; to having few wishes, not to having many wishes; to contentment, not to discontent; to seclusion, not to gregariousness; to the arousing of energy, not to indolence; to frugality, not to luxurious living' – of such things you can he certain: 'This is the Dhamma; this is the Discipline; this is the Master's teaching'.

Anguttara Nikaya, VIII, 53

Gotami, the aunt of the Buddha and the first nun he ordained, had gone to the Buddha requesting a pithy teaching that would help her when she was meditating in solitude in the forest. The Buddha's advice was to pay attention to the practical and transformative effects of her practice. Here we can see that the Buddha encouraged his followers to be self-reliant and that he believed that they could know for themselves if they were on the right track or not.

He told Gotami that the only thing she needed to do was to look at the effects on herself of the practice and teachings she was following. For the

Buddha the practice had to be transformative, it was not just a mechanistic ritual. The idea was to help people to diminish selfish desires, dissolve craving, weaken greed, lessen wants, reduce unhappiness, attenuate the urge to be distracted by other people, dispel laziness, decrease ostentation. A person's Dhamma was active and a matter of process. One can have faith in what one is practising and continue to practise in that way if it leads to experiencing more calm, more peace, to appreciating a simpler lifestyle, to being more self-confident and to having more energy.

These criteria require a certain amount of personal honesty and awareness of one's actions and being conscious of the results of these actions. Once I met a meditation teacher who told me that in his younger days when he used to meditate it made him angrier. When he finally realised this, he saw that he had misunderstood the instructions and was also applying them in the wrong way. He was using his times of meditation to repress himself and this in turn actually gave more energy to his negative tendencies. Once he saw this clearly, he totally changed the way he did meditation. And then it had a transformative effect and reduced his level of anger and irritation, and helped increase his kindness and patience.

> *There are also these five things that lead to the enduring of the Good Dhamma, to its not being forgotten and to its non-disappearance. What are the five? Here the bhikkhus and bhikkhunis and men and women adherents are respectfully devout towards the Teacher, towards the Dhamma, towards the Community, towards the Training and towards Concentration.*
>
> Samyutta Nikaya, XVI, 13

In this passage the Buddha, when asked by Kassapa, one of his main disciples, about the quality and the endurance of the Dhamma in the long term, explained that the transmission and furtherance of the Dhamma would depend upon the people who practised it. The Dhamma was not an entity separated from those who cultivated it. In order for it to continue, the Buddha suggested that his followers would need to respect the teachers, the teaching itself, the community, the training and concentration. Here again, the Buddha showed his pluralist approach-Cultivating one thing would not be enough to maintain the Dhamma. To esteem and listen to people who were more advanced and showed evident signs of accomplishment in terms of the three trainings of ethics, meditation and wisdom, was considered essential.

The followers of the Buddha needed also to appreciate and reflect on the teachings. If they were attentive towards each other as being part of the same community, whether monks, nuns, laywomen or laymen, this would also help the Dhamma to flourish. Moreover, the Buddha thought that cultivating and honouring ethical values was necessary for his tradition to be maintained healthily. And finally it was also essential to practise concentration and meditation for the Buddhist teaching to endure. So his teachings and practices were not dependent on a certain tribe, or a certain culture or certain rituals, or a certain time in history. They were dependent upon the people who practised them sincerely and were transformed by them, in turn impressing other people to practise and be transformed, and so on. In that way one could say that the Buddha's teaching became a world religion, which could adapt itself to different milieux, cultures and times.

AUTHENTIFICATION

Or a bhikkhu may say: 'In a certain dwelling place many elder bhikkhus live who are learned, expert in the traditions, memorizers of the Discipline, memorizers of the Codes; I heard it from those elders' own lips; this is the Dhamma, this is the Discipline, this is the Masters teaching....' Now such a bhikkhus' statement should be neither approved nor disapproved.... If, however, they are found to be verified in the Vinaya and confirmed in the Suttas, the conclusion to be made is this: 'Certainly this is the Buddha's word. It has been rightly learned by that bhikkhu or by that community or by those elders or by that elder'. You should remember these four principal authorities.

Digha Nikaya, 16

This passage comes from the *Maha-parinibbana Sutta*, which is one of the longest suttas and presents the last few months of the Buddha's life. In the final days of his life, the Buddha was trying to remind his followers of what was important and what was essential, and would teach it again and again. Here he was trying to help his followers after his death determine in what way they could know something was truly the words of the Buddha or in accordance with the teachings of the Buddha.

The Buddha suggested that one should not necessarily trust hearsay. It is not because someone said so that it was so. Somebody might hear the Dhamma from some respected elders or from someone else who has heard these respected elders, but this was not enough proof. The best way to ascertain if it was really the teaching of the Buddha was to check it against the vinaya and the suttas themselves. So the final arbiter was the teachings as compiled and memorised in the form of the vinaya and the suttas.

At the time the suttas could not be written down. They would be written down for the first time in Sri Lanka on palm leaves three hundred years later (first century BCE). There were, however, groups of monastics dedicated to memorising and transmitting the teachings of the Buddha orally. Different groups had the task of committing to memory a section of the Buddha's teachings. They would meet regularly to make sure they were remembering correctly the section they were responsible for. This is why as written texts the suttas are rather repetitive: the repetitions of certain portions of the texts were used as mnemonic devices.

The Buddha had noticed that after the early death of Mahavira, the great teacher of the Jains, his followers were arguing about his true teaching. It does not appear that they had thought of specific ways to conserve it while he was alive and teaching. Upon seeing this, the Buddha decided to put measures in place so that there was an oral record of his teaching which his disciples could put their trust in after his death. This is why groups of memorising monastics were formed.

In the year after the death of the Buddha it seems that a council was held and it is said that Ananda recited the suttas as he was famed for his accurate and phenomenal memory and had accompanied the Buddha for a long time. Upali is said to have recited the Vinaya. Scholars do not agree about the significance and total historicity of the first council. They do agree, however, about the historicity of the second council, also known as the Council of Vesali, which was convened because some monks did not seem to follow the Vinaya properly and were accepting money. At that council it was agreed that accepting money, gold or jewels was not proper for a monastic and that this was in accordance with the Vinaya as memorised orally. According to conjecture, after this council the monks who had not agreed with that decision decided to form a Buddhist non-canonical sect and in some way this was the start of the development of various Buddhist schools, an evolution that continues to this day.

A RAFT

So I have shown you how the Dhamma resembles a raft in being for the purpose of crossing over, not for grasping.

Majjhima Nikaya, 22 (abridged)

This passage refers to an episode when a group of monks had heard another monk say something about the Buddha's teaching that misrepresented it and in fact was the opposite of the Buddha's teaching. When they pointed out to the monk his faulty reasoning, he would not accept their criticism and continued asserting his wrong interpretation. So the group of monks called upon the Buddha for his thoughts on the matter. The Buddha agreed that indeed the monk had completely misunderstood what he had said about obstructions being obstructive, while the monk was claiming that they were not. But even the advice of the Buddha did not change the mistaken monk's mind or position.

It was at this point that the Buddha offered two similes about holding a snake and about using a raft. If one did not hold the snake in the proper way, it would bite one and cause one suffering. In the same way, if one did not understand the teaching correctly, the misunderstood teaching could bring harm. As for a wooden raft, it could help one cross over a river but there was no point in clinging on to it and carrying it everywhere with one. In the same way, the teaching was to help one cross over and should not be clung to. Moreover, the Buddha added that since one should not cling to a good teaching, there was all the more reason to let go of a false one.

Bhikkhus, the word of the Enlightened One is not to be rendered into classical metre. Whoever does so commits an offence of wrongdoing. I allow the Enlightened One's word to be learnt in one's own language.

Vinaya Mahavagga, Khandhaka 15

At the time of the Buddha, people in Northern India were speaking different languages. Vedic Sanskrit, the language of the sacred Vedas, was used mostly by the priests. Sanskrit was considered a higher language, while the colloquial languages were considered lower and were called prakrits. The Buddha is said to have talked in Magadhi. There is a great deal of controversy as to the true origin of Pali, the language in which the suttas have come down to us. Some scholars think that Pali might be a literary version of a certain prakrit form, possibly Old Magadhi. Since, however, the main source consists of inscriptions on Ashokan pillars, which are dated two hundred years later than the Buddha, the debate continues.

The Buddha wanted his teaching to be available to anybody. He did not wish to create a sect of specialists who would know a separate classical language and thus would be the only ones able to share and transmit a higher truth only accessible in that sacred language, as might have happened with the Brahmins and Brahminism and their use of Sanskrit. He hoped that his teachings could be understood by anyone and transmitted in ordinary popular language and dialects. Language was not to be a barrier and set a hierarchy. He did not consider that the words he used to teach had a special and sacred aspect separate from the meaning they conveyed. The main point was the meaning and the applicability of that meaning so that one could cultivate it and be transformed.

REFUGE

Ananda, I am now old, worn out, venerable, one who has traversed life's path, I have reached the term of life, which is eighty. Just as an old cart is made to go by being held together with straps, so the Tathagata's body is kept going by being strapped up. It is only when the Tathagata withdraws his attention from outward signs, and by the cessation of certain feeling, enters into the signless concentration of mind, that his body knows comfort.

Therefore, Ananda, you should live as islands unto yourselves, being your own refuge, with no one else as your refuge, with the Dhamma as an island, with the Dhamma as your refuge, with no other refuge. And how does a monk live as an island unto himself...with no other refuge? Here, Ananda, a monk abides contemplating the body as body, earnestly, clearly aware, mindful and having put away all hankering and fretting for the world, and likewise with regard to feeling, mind and mind-objects.

Digha Nikaya, 16

This passage also comes from the *Maha-parinibbana Sutta*. The Buddha had just been very ill but managed to recover somewhat and Ananda expressed his relief that he was better and that he could speak to his disciples again. But the Buddha pointed out to Ananda that this respite would be short-lived. The Buddha's body was conditioned like anyone else's and as he was eighty years old, it only kept going by fragile supports. For the moment, the conditions were kept in place and he could keep going. But it looks as though the Buddha knew he would not live much longer.

The Buddha was also telling Ananda that his body was in pain like anyone else's. Even so, he could deal with this excruciating pain by going into a deep state of concentration. Later over the centuries, the mythology of the Buddha as omniscient, perfect and totally impervious to anything after his awakening was to gain ground in the Buddhist editions. This passage, however, shows us that he was a human being who experienced pain like a common mortal, but because of his long experience of concentration practices he was able to go beyond it and experience himself in a different way. What he did was to remove his focus from his immediate environment and, as he stated in the *Culasunnatta Sutta,* 'without giving attention to perception of the base consisting of nothingness, without giving attention to perception of the base consisting of neither-perception-nor-non-perception, a bhikkhu gives attention to the single state (of non-voidness) dependent on (the presence of) the signless concentration of mind'.

In this important passage the Buddha is telling Ananda that since he, the Buddha, is going to die soon, Ananda must stop being dependent on him and instead must only depend on himself. Ananda must become an island and a refuge for himself, and the Dhamma must become an island and a refuge for him as well. The Pali term *dipa,* translated here as island, has also been translated as light. Nowadays scholars seem to think it is more likely to be island than light. The Buddha was telling Ananda that he could only count on himself to continue on the Buddha's way and apply the Dhamma. The Buddha is pointing out again that one must be self-confident and put one's trust in the teachings and hence in the practice of the teachings without the need for any intermediary.

Finally, the Buddha explained what he meant by taking refuge in oneself and in the Dhamma, and that is being mindful of the body, the feelings, the mind and the mind-objects. Again, this is not the transmission of a special secret metaphysical teaching, it is the transmission of a practice that can be carried out here and now and at all times. One just needs oneself and the intention to be attentive to what is happening inside and outside of oneself.

Here the Buddha did not say that after his death Ananda should follow such and such a person and consider him his successor, as the Buddha did not appoint any successor. The only thing that Ananda should follow was his own wisdom and the teachings of the Buddha. This well-known passage did not stop Buddhist traditions in the future from creating lineages that would be traced all the way back to the Buddha.

Chapter Nine

Continuity and
Transformation

THE ELDERS

'And what is the characteristic mark of good conduct?'

'It has as its characteristic that it is the basis of all good qualities. The five moral powers – faith, perseverance, mindfulness, meditation, and wisdom; the seven conditions of Arahantship – self-possession, investigation of the Dhamma, perseverance, joy, calm, meditation, and equanimity; the Path; readiness of memory (unbroken self-possession); the four kinds of right exertion; the four constituent bases of extraordinary powers; the four stages of ecstasy; the eight forms of spiritual emancipation; the four modes of self-concentration; and the eight states of intense contemplation have each and all of them good conduct (the observance of outward morality) as their basis. And to him who builds upon that foundation, O king all these good conditions will not decrease.'

'Give me an illustration.'

'Just, O king, as all those forms of animal and vegetable life which grow, develop, and mature, do so with the earth as their basis; just so does the recluse, who is devoted in effort, develop in himself the five moral powers, and so on, by means of virtue, on the basis of virtue.'

Milindapanha

The *Milindapanha* presents the conversations between a Buddhist monk Nagasena and King Milinda (Greek: Menander), who reigned in the second century BCE over an Indo-Greek kingdom in Northwest India. The text itself is supposed to have been compiled in the first century CE and might have been added to over time. The early Chinese translation of it has been found to be shorter than later Pali versions. Some scholars think that it might have been first written in Greek and then translated into Sanskrit, and later on into Chinese and Pali. This text is revered in the Theravada tradition of Southeast Asia (Burma, Sri Lanka, Thailand, Laos, Cambodia). It has even been incorporated in the official version of the Pali Canon in Burma even though it postdates the Buddha's time. The Theravada tradition is based on the teachings found in the Pali Canon. Theravada means school of the elders because this tradition is based on the earliest stratum of texts of the Buddhist tradition.

The Questions of Milinda is an interesting text, which shows us the way Buddhism was looked at and practised two or three hundred years after the death of the Buddha. It seems that it was still very much based on the teachings found in the Pali Canon and was recognisably Buddhist, with a definite emphasis on the three trainings of ethics, meditation and wisdom, with a specific importance given to ethics as the basis for the development of the other two trainings. This continued to be one of the main characteristics of the Theravada schools in the following centuries and up to the present time.

THE GREAT VEHICLE

For this reason, in emptiness there is no form, no feeling, no perception, impulse, consciousness; no eyes, ears, nose, tongue, body, mind....
The Heart of the Perfection of Wisdom Sutra

The Heart of the Perfection of Wisdom Sutra, generally abbreviated to *The Heart Sutra*, is a text widely used and studied in the Mahayana traditions of China, Korea, Japan, Vietnam and Tibet. It is an essential component of many Buddhist ceremonies and in South Korea it is recited at the conclusion of the thrice daily chants. As its longer name indicates, it belongs to the *Perfection of Wisdom* class of Buddhist Mahayana Literature (sometimes called the *Wisdom Discourses*). Some scholars think that it might have been adapted from translations in Chinese of longer versions of *Perfection of Wisdom* Sanskrit texts and then later translated from the Chinese back into Sanskrit. The first *Perfection of Wisdom* text was possibly written around 100 BCE and is considered one of the earliest Mahayana Sutras. More material in that genre was developed over the centuries. The first text had about 8,000 lines, and some of the following texts were expanded to 100,000 lines. The *Heart Sutra* (about 18 lines in all) is considered the quintessence or a summary of those longer texts and as such is very popular.

There is no unanimous accord among Western scholars about how, when or where exactly the Mahayana (literally 'Great Vehicle') arose. The word great, 'maha', qualifying a Buddhist school appeared around 383 BCE when the first schism in the Buddhist community happened. At what became known as the Council of Vesali, two factions arose, a liberal one and a more conservative one. The liberal group left and called itself the Mahasanghika (the great community). The other group became the Sthaviras (the elders). Over the centuries further dissension happened among the Sthaviras and various groups developed. It is thought that one offshoot of the Sthaviras tradition entered Sri Lanka, where it became one of the sources in the formation of the Theravada tradition.

The problem with the term Mahayana is that it implies there is a Hinayana (literally 'Small Vehicle'), but no Buddhist school calls or called itself 'Small Vehicle'. However, the Mahayanists applied the term Hinayana to all the early schools of Buddhism. In the beginning Mahayana and so-called Hinayana co-existed in India and then started to spread in various directions. Eventually the Mahayana traditions started to dominate in East and Central Asia. The early school-based teachings spread more slowly and later the term Hinayana was applied to the only remaining Pali-following school that called itself Theravada (the path of the elders) which grew in Sri Lanka and spread to Southeast Asia.

The Mahayana appeared in its more elaborate form in the second century C.E. The word Buddha means 'awakened'. It can mean the 'one who awakened (himself)' and, at the same time, the 'one who awakened (others)'. In these two possible definitions we could find the meaning behind the two terms – Hinayana and Mahayana – as employed by the Mahayana. Hinayana represented the Buddha as the ideal for those who wanted to awaken themselves. Mahayanists represented the Buddha as an example to those who wanted the liberation of others and thus the emphasis would be on the active cultivation of benevolence and compassion. In the Mahayana, the notion of the arahant was portrayed as meaning restraint, renunciation and self-awakening. In the Great Vehicle, the ideal of the realised being, the Bodhisattva, was awakening for the sake of all beings. The emergence of the Mahayana was also the decisive factor for great literary creative energy, and many different Mahayanist groups started to produce sutras in Sanskrit (sutta in Pali, sutra in Sanskrit) and attributed them to the Buddha in the belief that 'whatever is well-spoken is the word of the Buddha'.

The Mahayana tradition was a reform movement as well as the natural development of pre-Mahayana Buddhism. It is considered to be a continuation of earlier Buddhist doctrine and practices developed and expanded by creative thinkers and practitioners. In this passage from the *Heart Sutra* we can see suggestion of a sentence from a Pali discourse of the Buddha *(Kassaka Sutta)* where the Buddha said: '... Where no eye exists, no forms exist, no sphere of consciousness and contact at the eye exists....' In this passage the Buddha was expounding about the idea of non-grasping and not-self, and he finished his discourse by saying: 'What they speak of isn't mine.' He was pointing out that as long as one did not grasp at what one saw, heard, thought, and so on, as me and mine, one would be free. The Mahayanists took the notion of not-self formulated by the Buddha and expanded it into the notion of emptiness as ultimate reality of everything.

EMPTINESS

I have no body apart
from parts which form it;
I know no parts
apart from a 'body'.

Nagarjuna, Verses from the Center

Nagarjuna (around the second century CE) is an important philosopher in the Mahayana tradition. Little is known historically about him and there are many legends about him, the main one being that he lived for six hundred years. He is an important figure in Buddhism as he is considered the founder of the Madhyamaka School. This school rejected the notions of both eternalism and nihilism (like the Buddha) and advocated a middle path between the two, using the idea of emptiness as a means to do that. Up to the present times Madhyamaka teachings have influenced both

Tibetan Buddhism and the Zen traditions found in various countries in East Asia, though they might have different interpretations of those teachings. Nagarjuna is considered one of the ancestors of the Zen tradition (of which I will say more later on). His main achievement was to organise and expand the teachings found in the *Wisdom Discourses.* Many texts have been attributed to Nagarjuna, but his main work is *Verses from the Center,* from which this passage is taken.

Nagarjuna proposed that emptiness signified the absence of an essence in things but not their non-existence as phenomena. For Nagarjuna, emptiness is a characteristic of everything, meaning that anything that has arisen and exists lacks any intrinsic existence outside the causes and conditions that formed it. He saw form and emptiness as co-existent, as in this passage where he pointed out that his existence depended on his body. His body existed because of its parts, but each of the parts that constituted him was not the body in itself. Only when all the parts combined together did they institute a recognisable body. One could see Nagarjuna as the first deconstructivist as he tried consistently to take things apart and look at their constituents.

INTERPENETRATION

All lands are my body
and so are the Buddhas living there;
watch my pores,
and I will show you the Buddha's realm.

Just as the nature of earth is one
while beings each live separately,
and the earth has no thought of oneness or difference,
so is the truth of the Buddha.

Avatamsaka Sutra

The *Avatamsaka Sutra*, a seminal text for Mahayana Buddhism, was composed about five hundred years after the death of the Buddha and translated into Chinese in 418–420 by Buddhabhadra. It is an immense work of something like forty chapters. It is flowery and metaphysical, and the main themes are the interpenetration of everything and an explanation of the ten stages to attain awakening. In the life of the bodhisattva there are two essential moments: when he or she first gives rise to the mind of awakening by pledging himself or herself to attain supreme awakening for the benefit of all beings, and when he or she realises the supreme and complete awakening which makes him or her a Buddha.

A long gap can exist between these two moments as a bodhisattva must develop and pass through various stages to attain Buddhahood. At the beginning in India certain texts explained that they were four stages on the bodhisattva path. Later texts suggested a bodhisattva development in seven stages. Finally, a course in ten stages was accepted by most Buddhist schools. However, even with this analysis in ten stages there is not complete unanimity on the name and description of each stage. Different texts give different classifications.

With the *Avatamsaka Sutra* the teaching of the Buddha began to be transformed into a more metaphysical, and even a magical teaching at times. The texts produced are increasingly ornate and complex, with a multi-layered vision of millions of universes with countless radiant Buddhas. The ideas of the Buddha are taken to their utter limits. From the ideas of not-self and conditionality we are taken to the idea that since nothing is fixed and solid, everything is connected and so everything interpenetrates.

Two different and distinct tendencies will develop in connection with the original teachings of the Buddha. One tendency will be to take one word, or one sutra, or one idea, and build an exclusive tradition around it that will proclaim it has the only one and true teaching. And at the same time, traditions will regularly emerge that will try to create a synthesis of all the teachings available at their point in time. The last two lines of this passage from the Avatamsaka Sutra show us an early attempt at syncretism.

BODHISATTVA PRECEPTS

Refrain from praising yourself and slandering others

A disciple of the Buddha must refrain from praising himself and slandering others either by doing so himself or by causing others to do so. He must never create the causes and conditions for praising himself and slandering others, devise a means for doing so, or actually engage in such deeds himself. It is the duty of a bodhisattva to take upon himself the slander directed towards others, to transfer whatever is unpleasant to himself, and to give whatever is good to others. But if, on the contrary, a bodhisattva were

to make a display of his own virtue and wisdom and to conceal the virtues
of others thereby causing blame and slander to fall upon them (instead of
him), this would be an extremely serious transgression for him.

The Chinese Bodhisattva Precepts (Brahma's Net Sutra)

This is the sixth major precept of the ten major and forty-eight secondary
bodhisattva precepts as found in the *Brahma's Net Sutra*. It shows the
emphasis put on conditionality and intentionality in terms of ethical attitude
and thus this Chinese precept is the continuation of what the Buddha
taught. Then there is the relatively new notion of exchange of self for
others. Compassion is extended to create an attitude in which selflessness
is developed even further for the benefit of others.

Buddhism entered into China in the first century CE via the great caravan
route called the Silk Road that linked China with India. First Buddhist texts
had to be translated from central Asian languages or Sanskrit into Chinese.
Chinese translations started in 150 CE and continued at different times.
At the beginning there were two waves of translation activities. The first
translations were difficult and rather flawed as the foreign monks did not
really know Chinese and the Chinese translators did not know Sanskrit or
Central Asian language. These first translations were also strongly influenced
by Taoist terms. At first, Buddhism was seen as a kind of Taoism from the
Western Region. The need for more rigorous translations was recognised as
well as the necessity to find an appropriate Chinese vocabulary of Buddhist
terms that would be accurate and meaningful.

The second wave of translation (fifth and sixth centuries) was inaugurated
by the arrival in China of Kumarajiva (343–413 or 350–409), who is
traditionally considered the translator of the *Brahma's Net Sutra*. It is said
that Kumarajiva translated the Bodhisattva Precepts in 406 and that at that
time three hundred of his disciples received them. From 400 onwards,
what have been called 'original Chinese Buddhist sutras', often referred to
as apocrypha by scholars, started to appear in China. These texts were
created to respond to the needs of the Chinese people and to help them
benefit from the depth of the Buddhist tradition. These original Chinese
Buddhist sutras are composed of elements from traditional Buddhist sutras
mixed in with relevant and essential Chinese ideas.

The *Brahma's Net Sutra* is a good example of this kind of texts. Recently
scholars have come to an agreement that although the *Brahma's Net Sutra* was
traditionally assumed to be the tenth chapter of a lost Indian text translated

in 406 CE by Kumarajiva, it is actually a text composed in China between 440 and 480 CE. One of the main evidences for that hypothesis is the repeated appearance in the text of the two Chinese characters for 'filial piety and obedience' (fifteen times in all). Only original Chinese Buddhist sutras contain these characters. At the same time it looks as if it is a creative adaptation and expansion of a short portion of a sutra with the same title in the Pali Canon. In the Pali *Brahma's Net Sutra*, at the beginning the Buddha talks about minor, middle and major morality and his suggestions about morality are quite similar to the way the precepts are formulated in the Chinese *Brahma's Net Sutra*.

Some scholars think that it took two centuries for the *Brahma's Net Sutra* to be adopted by all Buddhists in China and to become the fundamental text it is now. Until the *Brahma's Net Sutra*, the lay followers and the monastics had taken different sets of precepts. The Bodhisattva precepts, being applicable to both and taken by both, fit in with the syncretist pattern of Chinese Buddhism and the universalist pattern of the Mahayana.

When the *Brahma's Net Sutra* came to Japan, the Bodhisattva precepts were adopted by the monks of the Tendai School in 822 as the standard discipline instead of the 250 precepts of the Dharmagupta Vinaya, which are adhered to by the monastics in China and Korea. Saicho (767–822), the founder of the Tendai School, felt the fifty-eight Bodhisattva precepts would be more relevant and adapted to the conditions of his times. Dogen (1200–1253), one of the seminal thinkers and exponents of the Soto Zen School in Japan, reformed the bodhisattva precepts further by restructuring them into the Sixteen Great Bodhisattva Precepts.

Two sets of Bodhisattva vows exist in Tibetan Buddhism, derived from Indian traditions. One set has slightly more vows than the Chinese version. In this set one finds eighteen root vows and fort-six branch vows. Some are quite similar to the one found in the *Brahma's Net Sutra*, but most of them are quite different. This shows how each Buddhist culture created ethics that fitted its own cultural condition and needs, but also accorded with the way they taught and practised the Dharma.

THE ZEN TRADITION

Emperor Wu asked: 'What is the highest meaning of the holy truths?'
Bodhidharma answered: 'Empty, without holiness.'
The Emperor said: 'Who is facing me?'

Bodhidharma replied: 'I don't know.'
The Emperor did not understand. After this, Bodhidharma crossed the
Yangtse River and came to the kingdom of Wei.

Blue Cliff Record, first case

Bodhidharma is reputed to have come as a monk from India in 479
to transmit the Buddhist teachings to China. After a long journey he
reached South China where he met Emperor Wu (502-550). The emperor
wanted to be given an explanation about the teaching of Bodhidharma.
Bodhidharmas reply, however, was succinct: 'Emptiness.' Furthermore, to
questions about his identity he replied that he did not know who he really
was. This is actually similar to the encounter between Nagasena and King
Milinda, who, when asked about his identity, did not affirm anything and
instead deconstructed and showed the parts that formed him. Here we
have the seminal founder of the Zen (Japanese; Chan in Chinese, Seon in
Korean) school in China, the Boddhidharma school, which is known for
its quick and short answers. We have the same discourse of conditionally,
impermanence and not-self, but with its own cultural modalities: abruptness,
pithiness, and a certain irreverence and demystification, one could almost
say desacralisation of the Buddhist teachings.

After this episode Bodhidharma is supposed to have crossed the Yangtse
river on a reed and reached the kingdom of Wei, and then went to a
mountain cave near Loyang where the Shao Lin Temple was later erected.
This temple has been made famous by Kungfu (martial arts) films, which
purport that Shao Lin-style Kungfu was started here by Bodhidharma.
Bodhidharma sat in a cave for nine years facing a wall. Buddhist scholars
have questioned many of the legends about Bodhidharma and even
questioned whether or not he existed. The consensus seems to be that
Bodhidharma should be seen more as a religious myth than a historical
figure. Scholars have also suggested that much of Zen history was created
over two centuries (650 to 850). It served the purpose of giving legitimacy
to the traditions and to inspire future generations. This is not considered
a cause of concern by most practitioners. For example, once the western
monks and nuns at Songgwang Temple in Korea suggested to Zen Master
Kusan that many Zen stories were historically untrue. The master replied
that it did not matter. For him, their truth did not depend on historical
accuracy. They had served the practitioners well over the centuries by helping
them to be provoked, inspired and awakened.

Early on, the Zen tradition claimed to be outside the scriptural tradition of the sutras, the recorded teachings of the Buddha, and commentaries about them. The practice was said not to require explanation. The only thing one had to do was 'to turn the light back onto oneself' in meditation and through that see one's own true nature. In doing so, one could be awakened and become a Buddha. Despite its insistence on direct experience, Zen has produced as many texts as any other Buddhist tradition. Throughout the centuries, however, meditation has remained the main emphasis.

> No-thought is to see and to know all things with a mind free from attachment. When in use it pervades everywhere, and yet it sticks nowhere. What we have to do is to purify our mind so that the six aspects of consciousness, in passing through the six sense organs, will neither be defiled by nor attached to the six sense objects.
>
> Hui Neng (683-713), *Platform Sutra*

After Bodhidharma, the Zen transmission is said to have gone to Huiko (around 485–553), then to Sengtsan (dates unknown) and Taohsin (580–651). Taohsin was followed by Hungjen (600–674), who was well known in his times and had many disciples in his monastery on Mount Huang Mei. It is with one of his disciples, Huineng (638–713), that Zen became established as a distinctively Chinese form of Buddhism. After Huineng, the teachings branched out and there started to be various lines of transmission, many of which continue to the present day. Each Zen master has a transmission booklet that has been given to him or her by their teacher when his or her awakening is recognised and 'sealed'. This process is called receiving 'Inka' (Dharma Seal). The booklet traces the line back generally all the way to the Buddha through the twenty-seven Indian patriarchs and the six Chinese patriarchs and the various Zen lines in China, Korea or Japan.

Huineng's *Platform Sutra,* in which his life and teachings are described, had a great influence on the Zen tradition and was even incorporated into the Chinese Mahayana Canon. In this passage 'no-thought' could be seen as the opposite of mindfulness as taught by the historical Buddha. If, however, we look at this quotation carefully, we see that 'no-thought' in Zen does not mean to have a blank empty mind, on the contrary it means to have a different type of operating mind: a mind that is aware of everything because it does not grasp at anything when the senses encounter the world. So here we have a traditional Buddhist teaching expressed in a Zen way.

> *However well you practise meditation, without moral discipline you will be like someone who is shown the way to a treasure house but never goes there. However well you endure austerities, without wisdom you will be like a person who intends to go East and heads for the West....*
>
> Korean Master Wonhyo (617–686 CE),
> *On Cultivating Determination to Practise*

Wonhyo, who founded the Dharma Nature School, was one of the most original thinkers in the history of Korean Buddhism. Buddhism entered Korea in the fourth century and in the following centuries five Buddhist doctrinal schools came into being. The Avatamsaka School and Won Hyo's school were two of the schools that had most influence on the future development of Zen in Korea as the ground was prepared for Zen to grow there. The Avatamsaka School took its name from the *Avatamsaka Sutra*, which also teaches that Buddhas and sentient beings are the same. Wonhyo's approach was syncretistic as he tried to create a sense of unity among the various trends of Buddhist thought at that time.

Wonhyo had a dramatic awakening as a young monk. On his way to China to find a teacher and learn more about Buddhism, he had to rest at night in a field after a tiring day. Everything was dark and he was very thirsty. Groping around him, he found a bowl containing water. It was fresh and thirst-quenching, and he felt that it tasted like nectar. The next morning when he woke up, in daylight he saw that he had slept in an old tomb and actually the bowl had been a shattered skull filled with stagnant water. He was shocked and repulsed. In that moment he realised that *'thinking makes good and bad, life and death. And without thinking there is no universe, no Buddha, no Dharma. All is one, and this one is empty. There was no need now to find a master'.* He then decided he did not have to go to China and turned back.

During the emergence of Zen in China, Koreans had been in constant contact with many of the leading Chinese Buddhist figures and Zen came to Korea around 630 CE. The first significant Korean Zen teacher was Toui (d. 825), who practised Zen in China for thirty-seven years. When he returned, the various doctrinal schools, each of them based on a certain sutra or one special Buddhist theory, were very powerful and their influence too strong for him to make any headway. His Zen teaching was too unorthodox with its idea of not relying on words and doctrines. The doctrinal traditions emphasised the importance of studying the sutras and gaining a clear understanding of the Buddha's teachings. This new Zen tradition, on the contrary, put the emphasis on realising the truth here and now through applying the Buddha's teaching by practising radical meditation.

After a while the simplicity and directness of Zen made it more popular and it was then that the influence of Wonhyo made itself felt. Instead of continuing the conflict with the doctrinal schools, a syncretistic approach organically emerged where the practice of Zen was provided with a solid theoretical underpinning. This is why this passage is interesting. It shows how Wonhyo encouraged people to cultivate equally the three trainings of ethics, meditation and wisdom as the Buddha had done before him. This is why to this day ethics is still important for the Zen tradition in Korea and the Vinaya is still adhered to by its Zen monks, whereas in the Japanese tradition it fell into abeyance and the monks became priests who follow sixteen precepts and are not necessarily celibate.

THE TIBETAN BUDDHIST TRADITION

Giving is founded on non-attachment. Moral practice is founded on reliance on spiritual friends. Patience is founded on humility. Effort is founded on meditation on death. Meditation is founded on dwelling in isolation. Wisdom is founded on mindfulness.

> Geshe Gonpapa in *Essential Advice*
> *of the Kadampa Masters*

Here, in this teaching from a Kadam master of the Tibetan tradition, we find essential Buddhist values – generosity, morality, patience, effort, meditation and wisdom – associated with qualities emphasised by the Buddha himself: non-grasping, spiritual friendship, humility, solitude, mindfulness. That effort is associated with meditation on death is interesting. The Buddha had suggested to his disciples that they should meditate in cemeteries and where the corpses were burnt. In the Tibetan tradition this was transformed into a meditative reflection on death.

In this method of meditation, one is told to focus and reflect on three essential points. First; one ponders the certainty of death. One thinks of all the people one knows or has heard about who have died. Secondly, there is the uncertainty of the time of death. One considers the fact that people die at different ages, and in different and unforeseen circumstances. Thirdly, one inquires into what, right now, are the most important things in one's life in light of the fact that death is certain but the time of its arrival uncertain. By reflecting regularly on death, one becomes more conscious of it and what it truly means – that at some point one will die. At first, this meditation might seem intellectual, but as one continues to practise one will find it becomes more experiential, something that one actually feels and that is not just a mental act. This practice changes the way one feels about death and the way one views life. Then it becomes more urgent and serious to meditate and so helps one to redouble one's effort.

The Kadam masters belonged to the Kadam tradition, which was founded in Tibet by the Indian Master Atisha (982–1054), who arrived in Tibet in 1042. Atisha and his followers thought that it was essential to cultivate the basic insights of Buddhism to develop a good ground before embarking on the secret tantric practices. The Kadam School had great masters and influenced some of the ideas of the four great schools of Tibetan Buddhism that remained in existence today, but the Kadam School itself did not exist for very long independently.

Buddhism entered Tibet from India officially during the reign of King Songtsen Gampo (born 605 or 617; reigned around 629–650). During the first four hundred years there was a great deal of interchange between Tibetan and Indian Buddhism. Tibetan monks went to India to study and many Indian teachers went to Tibet to teach Buddhism. Over time many texts were translated from Sanskrit and a Tibetan canon was created which included the early suttas, the Vinaya, but also numerous commentaries of Indian masters as well as texts produced by the Tibetans themselves. The Tibetans tried to organise all these texts in such a way that they could make sense of them in their entirety.

By the time it reached Tibet, Buddhism in India had developed in many different ways, currents and ideas over a thousand years. One of the trends that greatly influenced Tibetan Buddhism lay in tantric Buddhist ideas. Tantric Buddhist teachings are recorded in a series of texts called tantras. In Tibetan Buddhism the teachings and practices found in the tantras are called 'secret mantra' and those who follow tantric Buddhism are said to cultivate the 'Diamond Vehicle' (Vajrayana). The Diamond Vehicle is sometimes regarded by its own adepts as more elevated even than the Great Vehicle (Mahayana). Padmasambhava is considered the founder of Tibetan

Tantric Buddhism. There are many legends about Padmasambhava, but it seems that he came to Tibet in the ninth century. He was reputed for his magical powers and is said to have subdued many demonic forces, which were creating obstacles for the consolidation of Buddhism in Tibet.

Tibetan Buddhists, having received Buddhism quite late, were confronted with a myriad of teachings and practices. One of their major achievements was to organise these in such a way that they could be put all together. In Tibetan Buddhism one can therefore find Hinayana, Mahayana and Vajrayana co-existing peacefully and fitting with each other in such a way as to create a graduated path. Over time, four major schools developed: Nyingma, Kagyu, Sakya and Gelug.

In the same way as the hands and so forth
are regarded as limbs of the body,
likewise, why are living things
not regarded as limbs of life?

I should dispel the misery of others
because it is suffering like my own,
and I should benefit others
because they are living things, just like myself.
> Shantideva, *A Guide to the Bodhisattva's Way of Life*

Shantideva is an important figure because he is the author of *A Guide to the Bodhisattva's Way of Life*, a revered, much studied and practised text in the Tibetan tradition. Shantideva was a Buddhist master from the monastic Buddhist university of Nalanda in the eighth century CE. Nalanda had already existed as an important town in Magadha, not far from Rajgir, the capital of Magadha, and is mentioned as a staging post for the Buddha in the Pali suttas. In the fifth century CE a Buddhist university was created at Nalanda, which expanded vastly over the years. When the Chinese Buddhist pilgrim Hsuan Tsang visited it in the seventh century, there were ten thousand monks in residence belonging to different Buddhist traditions and from various countries. Many great teachers from Nalanda in its later period (ninth to tenth centuries CE) had a great influence on the development of Tibetan Buddhism. Nalanda was destroyed around 1197 by a Muslim invasion of Northern India.

The Buddha put great emphasis on compassion and harmlessness. In the *Guide to the Bodhisattva's Way of Life*, Shantideva developed these ideas and practices even further. In this passage he pointed out the equality of all beings already suggested by the Buddha. Suffering is painful to everyone, and in the same way happiness is appreciated by every single being. But Shantideva will expand this idea into the practice of replacing self by other and this is an intriguing part of the text when he asks the practitioner to put oneself in the other person's body and the other person in one's body and to consider various situations in that light. It is a challenging practice and reflection.

The blessings of the guru have entered my mind.
Grant your blessings so that I may realise my mind as shunyata.

Milarepa

Milarepa (1028/40–1111/23) is a highly esteemed teacher in the Tibetan tradition and considered one of the founders of the Kagyu School. The main concern of this school is the cultivation of tantric practices, and not getting lost in intellectual abstractions as was happening at the time of its foundation. This school is renowned for its three-year-long meditation retreats where people sit in a meditation box and never lie down to sleep. In a certain way it has a particular similarity to the Zen school with its emphasis on meditation practice and a certain carefulness about scholarly studies. One sees this movement again and again in the Buddhist tradition, increased scholasticism followed by a return to fundamental meditation practices.

Milarepa came from a wealthy family, but after the death of his father he and his mother were deprived of the family fortune by his father's family. Forced into poverty, he studied black magic to take revenge and managed to accomplish his vengeance by killing several people. Finally realising the gravity of his actions, he showed remorse and decided to practise Buddhism. Marpa, his teacher, made him undergo many hardships in order to purify him of his negative actions and their consequences. Milarepa became a great practitioner and spent much time in seclusion in remote caves and taught small groups of people through songs using the vernacular language.

This passage points out one aspect of the Tibetan tradition where there is a new way of looking at the teacher. At the time of the Buddha, the teacher was considered like a good friend, a guide, someone who had more knowledge and practice and could give indications, suggestions and would be an inspiration on the way. Over time in India, a new idea was developed about the teacher, that of the teacher as 'guru'. This was associated with the development of esoteric tantric practices. It was felt that to realise the goal of the Diamond Vehicle a profound devotion to one's spiritual master was essential.

In the Tibetan tradition, the teacher is seen as a guru or lama. He is considered to be performing the function of the Buddha himself. Any progress that one makes on the path is linked to the kindness and the blessing of the teacher. It is thought that without such a spiritual teacher who gained his wisdom from his own teacher who in turn received instructions from a lineage of others ancient masters, it is impossible to have any living access to the wisdom of the Buddhist tradition. The lama is often equated with the Buddha and sometimes is considered more significant for the student's actual practice than the historical Buddha. This is called guru yoga practice. One takes special vows in which one promises that one will not think badly of or criticise one's teacher. One must have total faith as one surrenders oneself to his or her higher wisdom. In this passage Milarepa was hoping that the blessing of his teacher, Marpa, would help him to realise emptiness (*shunyata*).

> *Buddhas say emptiness*
> *is relinquishing opinions.*
> *Believers in emptiness*
> *are incurable.*

Nagarjuna, Verses from the Center

Emptiness is a very important idea in the Mahayana, and yet at the same time Nagarjuna is pointing out in this verse that Buddhists have to use it in a careful way. The concept of emptiness is to help people to deconstruct their fixities and to dissolve the tendency they have to make things more solid and permanent than they might be. If, however, followers of the Buddha make emptiness into a thing that they grasp at, then it defeats the purpose of emptiness, which is of liberating them from their fixed views and habits.

> *In the daily activities of a student of the path, to empty objects is easy, but to empty mind is hard. If objects are empty, but mind is not empty, mind will be overcome by objects. Just empty your mind, and objects will be empty of themselves.*

Tahui, Swampland Flowers

In this passage from his letters to his disciples, Chinese Zen Master Ta Hio (1089–1163) made a similar point to that of Nagarjuna, that one has to handle emptiness carefully. It rejoins the Buddha's injunctions to use his teachings carefully or they might be more damaging than useful. Here Master Ta Hui is pointing out that it is relatively easy to see that objects are conditioned and impermanent and therefore empty. However, it is much harder to dissolve desires, ideas and grasping in the mind. If the mind is not empty of desires, aversions and lust, then the power of our impulses will be so strong that it will be easy for us to forget the emptiness of objects, and grasp at them or be overwhelmed by them. If, on the other hand, grasping has no roots in our mind, we will meet objects in a balanced and wise manner.

ZEN MEDITATION

Whether walking, standing, sitting or lying down, just constantly call the story to mind: 'Does a dog have a Buddha-nature or not? No.'

Tahui, *Swampland Flowers*

At the heart of Buddhist meditation one finds the two essential qualities of concentration and inquiry as taught by the Buddha. At the time of the Buddha, the main method was mindfulness, but over time various Buddhist traditions developed very different techniques of meditation. In the Zen tradition, two separate practices evolved: one using gongans (Chinese; gongan in Korean, koan in Japanese) and another one called 'silent illumination' or 'just sitting'. Gongans often depict an encounter between a Zen master and a disciple. The gongan is the whole story and the huatou (Chinese; hwadu in Korean) is the main point, which will be used as a question to focus on in meditation. Here Chinese Master Ta Hui is giving advice about the gongan 'No!'

Master Chaochou (778–897) experienced a profound awakening at an early age and following that trained for many years under his teacher before wandering all over China to deepen his understanding. When he was eighty, he settled in a small Zen temple in the town of Chaochou from which he took his name. After giving a talk in which he said that every sentient being had the Buddha-nature, Master Chaochou returned to his room. A monk followed him, and as he crossed the courtyard he saw a dog. The monk asked Master Chaochou: 'Does a dog have Buddha-nature, or not?' Chaochou replied: 'No!'

When one uses this type of Zen meditation, one repeatedly ponders: 'Does a dog have a Buddha-nature or not? No!' In Korea it is suggested that one asks: 'What was Chao Chou's mind before he said "No!"'? Or why did he say "No!"?' 'Or why "No"?' The concentration aspect is that one returns to the words of the question whenever one is distracted. The inquiry aspect is that one asks each question deeply. One asks because one does not know. It enables one's mind to become quieter and more flexible. Although it looks quite different from what the Buddha advocated, it has the same effect in that it makes one more aware in general as it loosens mental habits and it also makes one more conscious of impermanence and not-self.

The concept of Buddha-nature is a central tenet of the Mahayana tradition. It could have had its origin in a short text, the *Pabhassara Sutta* found in the *Numerical Discourses* (*Anguttara Nikaya*), where the Buddha mentioned that the mind can be luminous if free of defilements and that there is the possibility to develop it. It may be that Mahayana Buddhists found the idea of not-self too cerebral, and so the idea of Buddha nature might have emerged to give a more positive feeling about spiritual development. Over time this idea of Buddha nature was elaborated in many different ways along two main axes: either Buddha nature was emptiness, or it was not empty and thus corresponded to some kind of ultimate reality behind the illusory veil of appearance.

Nowadays Buddha nature is seen as the possibility within any being to awaken. Here there are two main schools of thought: either the awakening possibility is like a seed that one has to cultivate and develop, and that will bloom over time; or one is awakened already and one has to realise it here and now. Even with this idea, which is found in Zen traditions, there can be two further possibilities: either the actual awakening is covered by defilements that one has to remove over time to allow the awakening to shine; or the awakening is there already and there is nothing to do but to actualise it.

Silence is the primal stillness of the ground of the enlightened mind, whose natural activity is to shine.

Hungshi, *Cultivating the Empty Field*

The other Zen practice is that of silent illumination, which was introduced by Chinese Master Hungshi (1091–1157). Hungshi taught that awakening was to be experienced by sitting quietly, without focusing on anything special. In this practice, the maintenance of a firm posture is important and the mind meditates upon its own stillness. One tries just to be, to exist and be fully aware of that. The method of silent illumination is simply to sit and do absolutely nothing. To cultivate concentration one focuses on the moment itself, so that one is open to all its multitude of thoughts, feelings, sounds, tastes and smells. Inquiry enables one to be in the moment without being attached to it, without grasping, fabricating stories, daydreaming, regretting or planning. One just is – and in that instant one's mind can shine through brightly as Master Hungshi suggested.

TWO TRUTHS

Stainless meditation is done in a state of comprehending this Clear Light essence. It is free of mental darkness, agitation and fabrication, has no distraction and is beyond the conventional mind.

Longchen Rabjampa

Longchen Rabjampa (1308–1363/1369) was an important teacher of the Nyingmapa school of Tibetan Buddhism. It was the first Buddhist school to develop in Tibet after the introduction of Buddhism from India. Nyingma means 'the ancient ones' and this school connects itself back to Padmasambhava and to the first wave of Buddhism in Tibet. The three other schools were parts of the second wave, which took place at the end of the eleventh century after a dynastic breakdown in the ninth century that saw the disintegration of the Tibet Empire and the collapse of a central authority over the whole country. The Nyingmapa school sees the path in terms of nine vehicles or stages.

One of its primary teachings is that of Dzogchen (Great Perfection of Completion). It is considered by its followers as the highest and the most secret teaching of the Buddha. It involves the idea of a pristine, primordial awareness (i.e., great perfection) existing in all sentient beings. Moreover, the practitioners of Dzogchen think that to understand or have an indication about the nature of this primordial awareness, the mind-to-mind transmission of a highly realised master is essential. Although very different in its manifestation and expression, this view of 'great perfection' is quite similar to that of the school of Soto Zen. One of the practices associated with Dzogchen is that of sky-gazing; one sits, if possible outside in an open space, and gazes at the sky with the eyes wide open.

When Longchen Rabjampa mentioned 'conventional mind' he was referring to an idea which developed in Buddhism over time, that of relative or conventional and absolute or ultimate truths. The Buddha did not talk about relative and absolute truths. When people questioned him about how one could state what was true and only true and everything else was wrong, he was clear that it was very hard to find or demonstrate such absolute truth. In the end, what he thought could be truer was practice, experience and realisation of freedom from greed, hatred and ignorance as manifested by someone who had achieved this by reflecting and practising over a Period of time.

In some passages, however, the Buddha talked about speech that belonged to common and ordinary parlance, and speech that was more elevated and more in tune with the teachings about liberation from greed, hatred and ignorance. In other places he spoke of words that showed the Dhamma directly or indirectly. Scholars think that possibly from such passages the theory of the two truths was elaborated, moving from the distinction between conventional speech and elevated speech, or direct teaching and implicit teaching to conventional truths and ultimate truths.

The development of the two truths could also have come from an influence from the Indo-Greek milieu in which similar ideas were also brewing at the time. In the Theravada tradition, over time what was conventional was everything apart from consciousness, mental factors, matter and nibbana. In the Mahayana tradition, where the theory of the two truths is essential, one can find two views. One is that everything is conventional apart from emptiness, which is of the order of ultimate truth. On the other view, everything is conventional apart from the supreme awareness, which is behind all things.

Some Buddhists think that ultimate truth is superior to conventional truth and some think that they are complementary, that they are two different ways of looking at the world. For example, I have a relative sense of self, resulting from the conditions that form it, and at the same time this self is empty of inherent existence. At one level it looks relatively there and functioning, and at another level it is a chimera. I think that the main idea of the two truths is to help us deconstruct our fixed views and an attempt to see the world in a more multi-perspectival context. It is in any case true that it has also become like an article of faith and can lead to some relatively rigid positions for some Buddhists.

LOVING WORDS

Loving words means to address all sentient beings affectionately with your heart full of compassion. Regard them as your own children. Praise the virtuous and speak kindly to the wayward. Overcome bitterness and hatred with loving words and establish friendship with all. Loving words brighten the spirit and warm the heart.

Dogen, *Shobogenzo*

By the time Dogen wrote these words, 1700 years separated him from the Buddha's time, but here we find the same emphasis on compassion, kind speech and empathy. Dogen (1200–1253), the founder of the Soto Zen tradition in Japan, is one of the more important Buddhist figures in that country. He was born in an aristocratic family but his parents died when he was very young. Being struck by the awareness of impermanence at such an early age, he decided to become a monk at thirteen. Very soon he was plunged into perplexity by the question posed by the idea of Buddha nature in the Mahayana tradition: *'If all beings originally possess the Buddha nature, why does one need to engage in practices to realise it?'*

Someone suggested he should go to China and study in the Zen school to find an answer. First he went to some temples where they studied the gongans but he felt they put too much emphasis on illogical actions and words while discarding the deep meaning of the Buddhist suttas. He was going to give up and return to Japan when he was sent to master Juching (1163–1228). Juching believed that Zen was *'dropping away body and mind'* – that is, forgetting our body and mind, not being so attached to our ideas, pains and pleasures. He taught *zhigandazu* (Chinese; *Shikantaza* in Japanese, 'just sitting') as a form of meditation. As one sat, one did not try to answer any questions or riddles nor try to gain awakening. Dogen received the Dharma Seal from Master Juching.

He returned to Japan in 1227 and in the next few years wrote many of his important works such as *Instruction for the Tenzo (Head Cook)* that are still followed in temples all over Japan, and he started to expound some of the fascicles of *Treasury of the True Darma Eye (Shobogenzo)*. Dogen died at the age of fifty-two in 1253. Dogen put great emphasis on the posture while one sat in meditation and ascertained that sitting still, *zazen,* was enlightenment itself. Dogen was nearly forgotten, even in his own school, over the centuries until he was rediscovered in the 1800. As in Japan, so in all the other countries where Buddhism spread, many schools, theories and practices developed through the impulse of people, men and women, who cultivated the spirit of the Buddha and adapted it or recreated it to evolve with the culture, history, geography and the different conditions in which they found themselves. So the spirit of the Buddha survived to reach and find itself in modern times and what we find now shows clearly that Buddhism too is conditioned, impermanent and creative.

Chapter Ten

Modern Times

MINDFULNESS OF THE BREATH

Keep your attention on the breath. Perhaps other thoughts will enter the mind. It will take up other themes and distract you. Don't be concerned. Just take up the breathing again as your object of attention.

Ajahn Chah, Bodhinyana

Ajahn Chah (1918–1992) was a great Thai master of the twentieth century. He became a monk at the age of twenty-one. Upon entering the monkhood he studied Buddhist doctrines and the Pali language. After his father's death, he felt the need to put into practice what he had learnt and went to practise meditation with one of the great meditation teachers of his time, Ajahn Mun. Thereafter he followed the austere path of the Forest Tradition. After wandering and meditating in the countryside and the jungle for seven years, he established a temple called Wat Bah Pong.

In 1966 a young Westerner, who had recently been ordained under the name of Sumedho, came to practise under him. Other Western followed, so many that a special temple for foreigners was built called Wat Nanachat. Later these Western monks and nuns returned to the West, created various temples all over the world, and followed the Thai Forest tradition. The Thai

Forest Tradition was revived at the beginning of the 1900s in Thailand as a way to go back to the original source of the Buddhist tradition – ethical discipline based on the Vinaya and meditation.

In this quoted text, Ajahn Chah is giving advice on how to practise meditation on the breath, one of the foundational meditation practices in the Buddhist tradition. This technique, which has come down to us through the centuries, has been explained and cultivated in different ways over time, but it has always been based on, and extrapolated from, the *Satipatthana Sutta (The Foundations of Mindfulness Discourse)*. He is pointing out that it is natural to be distracted when trying to focus on the breath by all kind of thoughts, but one should not be excessively committed to these trains of thoughts. One can let them arise and pass away, and returning to focusing on the breath will help one to let go of them more easily.

MINDFULNESS OF FEELING

Studying feeling, we concentrate on what it is, what its characteristics are, until, through meditation, we realise it is nothing at all. It is merely coming and going under impermanence, suffering and not-self. It is important to see the deceit of 'feeling', that it is just deceiving us all the time.

Ajahn Ranjuan

Ajhan Ranjuan is a Thai meditation teacher who was ordained late in life but mastered meditation quickly and was encouraged to teach early on by her teacher, Venerable Buddhadassa. When I met her she was teaching a retreat for a hundred people but gave me all her time as if she had nothing else to do. Her eyes radiated an amused kindness, she felt like the epitome of compassion and attentiveness. Her status was ambiguous – she had a shaved head and wore black and white instead of all-white as Thai nuns do. She said she was more like a lay woman, though she seemed to me more like a nun when I met her in 1992.

Although the Buddha did not see any obstacles preventing women from attaining awakening and he let women receive ordination, over time the culture of patriarchy in which Buddhism found itself did influence its egalitarian tendency, and the supremacy of men over women developed. This did not mean that great Buddhist women and nuns did not exist over the centuries, but they were less celebrated and less influential than the men.

Modern times with access to secular education, human rights and remunerated work allowed women to become more equal and respected in their societies and the same happened in Buddhism, in the East and the West. Nowadays one will find many women practising and teaching Buddhism and meditation. Ajhan Ranjuan, although very humble, is one of them. In this quotation she is suggesting that, as the Buddha pointed out, it is important to examine and be aware of feelings because of the way we are taken over by them and assign greater value and importance to them than is necessary.

She is coming back to the three characteristics as stated by the Buddha, that however real and powerful a feeling seems to be, it too is conditioned, unreliable, likely to cause suffering if grasped at. She is encouraging us to see the evanescent nature of feelings, which come and go. They do not exist independently of the various conditions that give rise to them. If we can see this with the help of meditation, we can learn to develop a different attitude towards feelings that will enable us to engage with them creatively instead of being overpowered or paralysed by them.

SOCIALLY ENGAGED BUDDHISM

The Buddha taught social freedom, intellectual freedom, economic freedom, and political freedom. He taught equality, equality not between man and man only but equality between man and woman. It would be difficult to find a religious teacher to compare with Buddha, whose teachings embrace so many aspects of the social life of a people, whose doctrines are so modern, and whose main concern was to give salvation to man in his life on earth, and not to promise it to him in heaven after he is dead.

Dr Ambedkar, *On Buddhism*

Dr Ambedkar (1891–1956), an untouchable himself, became a leader for India's untouchables in the decades leading up to Indian Independence. He became India's first law minister after independence. He was also one of the main architects of the Indian Constitution. He was a great reader and studied the early Buddhist suttas at length. In devising a new constitution he was influenced by the way the early Buddhist monastic community conducted its affairs – voting by ballot, following certain rules of debate, the use of precedence and also of agendas and committees. This

Buddhist model was itself based on the governing way of the republic of the Licchavis.

All through his life Dr Ambedkar was critical of the discrimination the untouchables had to endure and he kept looking for a way to take them out of the rigid Indian caste system. For many years he studied Buddhism in depth. Finally, in 1956 he converted to Buddhism and organised the mass conversion to Buddhism of a large group of untouchables, thereby changing their status. He died a few weeks later, but his legacy is still alive today in India.

When he studied the suttas, Dr Ambedkar was looking for a way to liberate his people. In the text quoted above he explained what he found in the Buddha's teachings that inspired him to choose Buddhism as a means for his people to escape discrimination and to help them rebuild their self-esteem and lead worthwhile lives. His motto was 'Educate, organise and agitate'. He felt that the teachings of the Buddha would provide a good basis for the untouchables to develop themselves in a positive, modern and not delusive way, now, in the present, especially because it was not based on the idea of going to a future paradise after their death.

VISUALISATION

Let us now visualize Arya Chenrezig at the centre of our heart, about the size of a thumb. He is either two-armed or four-armed, seated on a lotus on top of a moon-disk. He is the essence of all the Buddha's wisdom and compassion. He is our true nature, the essence of our mind.

Tenzin Palmo, *Reflections on a Mountain Lake*

Venerable Tenzin Palmo was born in 1943 in England and has been a Buddhist nun for about forty-four years. She was one of the first Western women ordained in the Tibetan Buddhist tradition. She went to India in 1964 and spent a total of twenty-four years there. She spent six years in Dalhousie with her lama teacher, eighteen in Lahul, six in her lama's monastery and twelve in solitary retreat in a cave. She returned to Europe to live in Assisi in 1988. In 1992 people suggested she should build a nunnery in India.

Venerable Tenzin Palmo had been concerned for many years about the poor state of education and practice opportunities for Buddhist nuns of the Tibetan tradition in India. For this project, she took up travelling and teaching to raise funds. In 2000 the Dongyu Gatsal Ling Nunnery was opened to Buddhist nuns from the Himalayan regions. In 2008 she received the title of Jetsunma, the highest honorific title you can give to a nun or a laywoman in the Tibetan tradition.

In the quoted text Venerable Tenzin Palmo is explaining in simple terms the method of Tibetan Buddhist visualisation. The idea is to visualise a complex three-dimensional image or *mandala*. To hold this image, full of detail, in your mind for any amount of time requires a high level of concentration. At the centre of the *mandala* there is usually an image of a Buddha or deity who embodies a certain enlightened quality such as wisdom or compassion. While you are visualising the image, you imagine yourself to be that Buddha, sharing his degree of understanding and love. In this case it is the visualisation of the Bodhisattva of compassion called Chenrezig in Tibetan and Kuanyin in Chinese. What is interesting is that in the Tibetan tradition the Bodhisattva of compassion is male and in the Chinese tradition she is described as female.

THE GRADUATED PATH

In the first type of discerning meditation, we seek to transform our attitude. When meditating on love, the object of meditation is other beings. We consider their kindness towards us in the past, present and future.
Thubten Chodron, *Open Heart, Clear Mind*

Venerable Tubten Chodron is an American Gelugpa nun from the Tibetan tradition. She was born in 1950 and became a nun in 1977 at the age of twenty-seven. She has been a nun for thirty-one years. In 1986 she went to Taiwan to receive full ordination. The full ordination for nuns disappeared in some Buddhist countries like Sri Lanka and never reached other countries like Tibet. In the Tibetan tradition nuns can only receive lower ordination and so have a lower status and fewer opportunities. In Sri Lanka the full ordination was re-instated in 1996 with the help of concerned Sri Lankan monks, Western nuns, the Taiwanese and Korean Buddhist monastic communities, where the full ordination for nuns was transmitted and exists to this day.

Venerable Tubten Chodron has played a crucial role in trying to establish the full ordination in the Tibetan tradition and was instrumental in 2007 in the setting up in Berlin of the First International Congress on Buddhist Women's Role in the Sangha, Bhikshuni Vinaya and Ordination

Lineages, with the Dalai Lama in attendance. She is the abbess of Sravasti Buddhist Temple in Washington State. She is very active in promoting monasticism, participating in inter-faith monastic dialogue, and in creating Buddhist programmes for people in prison.

In this quotation she is presenting the graduated path to awakening; also known as Lam Rim, which is an essential component of the practice in the four schools of Tibetan Buddhism. In the Gelugpa tradition it is implied that only after cultivating the graduated path can one embark upon the cultivation of Vajrayana practices. This graduated path is the systematic introduction to Buddhist doctrines as a path of reflections and practices. There are hundreds of different 'Stages on the Path' (Lam Rim) developed by various teachers over the centuries. In the Gelugpa tradition, the first stage is the cultivation of guru devotion to develop confidence in the teacher and his teachings.

Then there are the stages following the three different types of motivation – inferior, middling and superior. These three levels are structural devices to indicate the path in the three primary levels of practice as understood in Tibetan Buddhism. The idea is to go through all the three levels of motivation without jumping a level. In one's daily meditation, one starts to reflect on all three levels at a glance so as to create a context for further specific analytical meditations and reflections.

The first level helps people to recognise the suffering of samsara and inspire them to develop the motivation to want to improve their destinies by gaining a favourable rebirth. One analytical meditation at this level is to reflect on death – the certainty of it, the uncertainty of its time, and what is important in the face of it. At the second level, people recognise that no rebirth will ever be permanent and that the only solution is to develop the motivation to cut off the cycle of birth and death and to attain nirvana. At this level the analytical reflections focus on suffering and the causes of suffering, for example.

In the third level, people recognise that not only they themselves but also all sentient beings suffer the cycle of birth and death. So the only way to bring this greater suffering to an end is to have the motivation to become a bodhisattva or a Buddha who will not enter nirvana until all sentient beings themselves are liberated from samsara and enter nirvana. Here one will meditate on exchanging self for others or try to cultivate the six perfections (paramitas) of generosity, morality, patience, effort, concentration and wisdom.

Ven. Thubten Chodron once said that she liked the graduated path because she found that it helped the mind to think constructively through its analytic, checking form of meditation. Here she explains a certain type of meditation where the aim is to develop love for other beings. In order to develop love and compassion, one first needs to focus on others in a specific way, not at random, but focusing on the good things that they might have done for us. We often think negatively about ourselves and others. Here we have a meditation that makes one reflect in a concrete way about the kindness of others. The more we reflect in this way, the more our heart will be suffused with love for ourselves and others (simply put, if people are kind to us, we are not so bad, and if they are kind, they are not so bad either).

MENTAL DISTRACTIONS IN MEDITATION

We sit, expecting that this self, which chases after ideas and things, is meeting its end, yet stray thoughts come up again and again. Every time we realise that we have been riding a train of thoughts back to England or off to America, we return to our sitting. We must awaken the desire for enlightenment. Billions of times we realise we have wandered off, but all we need do is return to our bodhi mind and our sitting.

Aoyama Roshi, *Zen Seeds*

Aoyama Roshi is the Zen abbess of a large training centre for nuns of the Soto tradition in Japan. She is a renowned writer and expert in the art of tea and flower arrangement. She is also involved in monastic interfaith dialogue. Here again she points out like Ajahn Chah that when we sit in meditation we will not be free from distracting thoughts. When we meditate in the practice of the Zen, Theravada, Tibetan or other Buddhist traditions, we will be plagued by thoughts.

The thoughts are not produced by the meditation but by the habits of mind. Often people are anxious about all these thoughts, and discouragement could gain the upper hand. However, Aoyama Roshi is pointing out that the amount of thoughts and the kinds of thoughts do not matter. What is essential is to come back to the sitting, to the body sitting on the cushion, to the mind which is trying to concentrate, to the potential of our Buddha nature in each moment.

PURE LAND BUDDHISM

*You must practise in your heart. After you believe in the Pure Land
outside, you will believe there is the Pure Land in your heart. Finally,
you will see the world as the Pure Land. You know there is America
although you have never been there, but you know one day you will
go there. It is the same with the Pure Land.*

I Itsao

Venerable I Tsao is a Taiwanese nun and a practitioner of the Pure Land
tradition. She is a member of a large temple situated in the south of Taiwan
called Fokwangshan, which is like a Buddhist living mandala from cradle
to grave. There are an orphanage, several kindergartens, junior and high
schools, several Buddhist colleges, graduate courses, a hospital, a retirement
home and a funeral parlour. It is quite a large complex spread over several
green and lush hills. The clinic has one doctor, a layman, three nurses,
laywomen, and a few nuns who have trained as nurses as well. It is free
and the people come from around the area. There are also a dentist and
an optometrist. In the funeral parlour there are urns kept specifically for
poor people because it can be quite costly to get a place for an urn. In
between there is a hospice.

There are five departments at Fokwangshan: educational (for sangha),
superintendence/administration (branch offices, matters concerning devotees),
cultural (publishing works/speeches), sangha (sangha matters, illness, going
abroad for higher education, benefit of society), compassion foundation
(poor people/ambulances going to remote villages to give medicines free).
In the retirement home there is one block for men, one for women and
one for couples. Some people become monks and nuns and shave their
head after they have stayed there for a while. There can be 120 people in
all. Ten people on the staff are paid and there are quite a few volunteers.
There is also a prison-visiting programme. Fokwangshan, although special
because of its size and vast development in Taiwan and abroad, is a good
example of a typical modern Buddhist temple, active in many different
areas, spiritual, educational and compassionate.

Although the ordination lineage of Fokwangshan comes from the Linchi
Chan School, many people there cultivate Pure Land practice. The Pure
Land tradition was founded in 402 by the Chinese monk Huiyuan, who
stressed the importance of the mythical Buddha of light, Amitabha, who

resides in a Pure Land known as the Western Paradise. The objective of the Pure Land believers is to be born in this Pure Land in order to be in the presence of Amitabha Buddha. Master Huiyuan devised the simple practice of reciting the name of Amitabha Buddha. This practice can be found in many Mahayana Buddhist traditions and countries. While, as Ven. Itsao pointed out, there is the aim to be reborn in the Western paradise, it has to be recognised that the here and now becomes the Pure Land. This leads to both an inner and an outer transformation. One tries to see everything as the Pure Land and one also tries to do all one can to transform the world to become like a Pure Land.

THE SHINGON TRADITION

I find the Shingon meditative tradition and techniques to be very dynamic; there is this constant inner change and flow of energies and images. What takes place in some of the meditative states is developing an ability to look at our intentions and actions, and those of others, much more clearly.

Eko S. Noble

In 1992 Venerable Eko S. Noble lived in Daifukuji, a Shingon temple, which is situated near Nara, an ancient capital of Japan. At that time two nuns lived there, a Japanese and a Westerner. Venerable Tairyu was eighty-eight years old and had been in this temple for fifty years. In October 1992 Venerable Eko, an American, had just arrived to become the head nun so that Venerable Tairyu could retire as she was ill. Later Venerable Eko went back to the USA to teach. Shingon is a Buddhist Japanese esoteric tradition, similar to the Tibetan tantric tradition, which uses recitations of sacred syllables (mantras), special hand gestures (mudras), visualizations of mandalas, and the use of fire in rituals.

This Buddhist tradition was founded by Kukai (774–835) and centred on the figure of Vairocana Buddha. Vairocana Buddha is one of the early Buddhas who was developed by the Mahayana as a symbol of ultimate reality. Vairocana means the luminous one. He is seen as representing Buddhism's profound doctrines on emptiness and the interpenetration of all things. The practices of this Japanese tantric tradition are quite remote from what was advocated by the Buddha 2500 years ago. All these developments responded to certain needs of the people at that time and came out of the creative impulses of the teachers who made the changes. The tradition has continued to this day because some people have been inspired by these esoteric teachings and have been able to apply these techniques successfully. In the end, it seems to have a similar effect to other types of Buddhist methods, as Venerable Eko explained, that of enabling people to be more aware and so to be more creatively engaged with themselves and others.

THE TIEN TAI SCHOOL

It is important to understand the state of 'quietness and liveliness'; if you do not, you cannot understand meditation. It is important that our meditative state of mind should be very clear and lively.... T'ien T'ai teaches you how to use your mind, not to control your mind.

Hiu Wan

Venerable Hiuwan was a Chinese nun of the T'ien T'ai School. When I met her in 1992, she was an active eighty-one-year-old, a painter, a meditation master, a scholar and an educationalist. She had arranged for a large technological college to be built near Taipei in Taiwan. Born in China in 1913, she attended art colleges in mainland China and Hong Kong. In the 1940s she studied at Tagore University in India and stayed at the Aurobindo Ashram in South India. In the 1950s she went on a round-the-world trip for three years, holding exhibitions, and teaching meditation and Chinese art. Upon returning she became a nun and decided to dedicate her life to promoting Buddhist education, art and literature. She came to Taiwan in 1967 to lecture on Buddhist philosophy and art, and founded the Lotus Buddhist Ashram in 1970. In 1980 she founded the Institute for Sino-Indian Buddhist studies, which offered graduate courses.

The T'ien T'ai Buddhist tradition, which is considered a specific Chinese creation and later was further developed in Korea and in Japan, is interesting for its attempt at integrating both Pali suttas and Mahayana sutras in its doctrine. It was founded by Chih-i (538–597), who divided the Buddhist tradition in five periods and eight teachings that would culminate in the teaching found in the Lotus Sutra. Chih-I advocated a combination of study and practice of meditation. He put a special emphasis on the training of the mind. He wrote a meditation text entitled 'Great Concentration and Insight' where he showed how to cultivate together concentration (samatha) and insight (vipassana), which was one of the main teachings of the Buddha. As Venerable Shig Hiu Wan reminds us, concentration is an essential element of meditation as it helps us to develop quietness, and at the same time it is important to cultivate it together with insight or experiential investigation, which will enable us to become clearer and livelier.

MODERN BUDDHISM

It seems to me that when we fall ill, we have an opportunity we may not have noticed when we were well, to literally in-corp-orate the wisdom of the Buddhas, and to present it as our own body.

Darlene Cohen, *Being Bodies*

Nowadays the Buddha's teachings and meditation practices have been widely disseminated in the Western world. A new wave of disciples of the Buddha is applying his advice in a modern and practical context. Darlene Cohen is a case in point. She is an American Zen priest and meditation teacher who trained in the USA under teachers who had received their Zen transmission from Japanese priests who had come to live in the USA. She wrote a book called *Finding a Joyful Life in the Heart of Pain* because she had suffered from rheumatoid arthritis for twenty-three years and found that her meditation background and the Buddha's teaching helped her to deal with chronic pain.

Her main recommendations are to 'acknowledge pain and its burden and enrich one's life exponentially'. She feels that when one is in chronic pain, instead of fleeing the pain one needs to know it deeply and acknowledge the suffering it is causing and at the same time balance this by developing one's potential for happiness and discovery, 'making it so rich that no pain can commandeer it'. She points out that when we are in chronic pain we can have a tendency to grasp at the past that was not painful and thus negatively grasp at the present which is painful. In this way, instead of dealing with the pain effectively, we are actually reinforcing it. When she finally accepted fully her rheumatoid arthritis and 'the body she had to live the rest of her life with', she felt a sense of release and more peace.

In exploring how we each might personally act in the world, it is first very important to realise that what the world most needs are our unique contributions, our own individual ways of living an engaged spiritual life, rather than our performances of some imagined set of uniform duties.

Donald Rothberg, *The Engaged Spiritual Life*

One of the developments of the spirit of the Buddha in the modern world has been its application in a variety of ways to the lives of lay people outside the traditional monastic context. People feel that one of the Buddha's main messages is that of non-harming and compassion, and so they want to cultivate right action, one branch of the eightfold path, as compassionate and helpful action. As a result, a strong movement of 'engaged Buddhism' has developed in the West. Throughout the centuries, whenever it has been possible, Buddhists have tried to cultivate and develop compassionate activities. In the past, monks and nuns were often at the forefront of this movement, and often still are in the East, though this is changing there as well. In the West, however, Buddhist lay people are becoming more involved not only in teaching but also in social action. Donald Rothberg, who is representative of this movement, is a meditation teacher and has been a board member of the Buddhist Peace Fellowship.

The fact that lay people, men and women, are more involved with teachings and social action is due to various reasons, but the main two seem to me to be that monasticism is not widespread in the West and that with modernity Western Buddhist lay people have been able to be educated and take holidays or time out from their work. Education means that the study of the Buddhist texts is no longer the preserve of the monastics. Holidays enable lay people to go on long meditation retreats as the monastics can do and thereby achieve the same proficiency in study and meditation as the monastics, even if they live a lay life.

Buddhist monasticism, which implies celibacy as in Thailand and Korea, has some Western adherents, but it is not a large movement yet because it necessitates a large financial infrastructure to support a certain body of monks and nuns. The Japanese priesthood, in which people can marry and work at ordinary jobs, is easier to sustain financially. The celibate Western Buddhist monks and nuns are well respected and admired, but their choice is considered by many a special vocation, not entered upon lightly. Many people find it easier to follow the spirit of the Buddha as a lay person. Many laymen and laywomen have emerged as good teachers and scholars.

The ultimate aim of the Mindfulness-Based Cognitive Therapy program is to help individuals make a radical shift in their relationship to the thoughts, feelings, and bodily sensations that contribute to depressive relapse, and to do so through changes in understanding at a deep level.

Segal, Williams and Teasdale; *MBCT for Depression*

Another interesting development in modern times has been the encounter between psychology or psychotherapy and Buddhism. A few psychologists and psychotherapists have taken up Buddhist meditation and some Buddhist meditators have become psychologists and psychotherapists. People have been struck by the fact that one can find systems of Buddhist psychology in the Theravada tradition and the Tibetan tradition. The most recent and widespread development in this field has been the use of Buddhist mindfulness meditation in association with stress reduction, as taught by Jon Kabat-Zinn, and then later on with cognitive therapy.

The quotation above is a case in point. Its authors, Mark Williams, John Teasdale and Zindel Segal, who all specialised in studies of psychological models and treatment of depression, were asked to develop a maintenance programme of cognitive therapy to prevent further relapse for people who had had several episodes of depression. Cognitive therapy was chosen as it was one of the therapies found to be as effective as anti-depressant medication when dealing with depression. In the course of their research, Mark Williams, John Teasdale and Zindel Segal decided to bring in the mindfulness approach of Dr Jon Kabat-Zinn to complement the cognitive techniques. Over the course of a few years they developed what is now known as a Mindfulness-Based Cognitive Therapy (MBCT) programme for depression, an eight-week course for groups of patients who have suffered several occurrences of depression.

There seem to be many common points between Buddhist practice and cognitive therapy. They deal with the same material – human suffering and how to relieve it. They have in common a pragmatic approach that sees and finds a deep value in acceptance and compassion. Dr Aaron T. Beck, one of the founders of cognitive therapy, believes that they share a commitment to 'self-responsibility' and that both methods focus on the 'immediate', and 'try to separate distress from pain and use mindfulness training'.

When I read the book on MBCT, I was struck by the fact that the course that had been developed was totally in accordance with the four great efforts as taught by the Buddha:

- To cultivate conditions so that negative states that have not yet been created do not arise
- To let go once the negative state is present
- To cultivate conditions so that positive states have the possibility to appear

• To sustain positive states once they are there

During the eight-week course the participants are taught various techniques of awareness, mindfulness, inquiry and concentration, with an emphasis on awareness in the body as a means to take the focus and energy away from the negative mental ruminations which in combination with low moods will trigger a depressive state. People are encouraged to explore, accept and let go of their negative feelings and thoughts, and to recognise and build on the good feelings, capacity for joy and ability they have in order to accomplish something of value and meaning.

The spirit of the Buddha in modern times has many aspects, and following the teachings of conditionality of the Buddha, it has influenced modernity as much as it has been influenced by modernity.

Glossary

Chi. = Chinese
Kor. = Korean
Jap. = Japanese
Pal. = Pali
Skt = Sanskrit
Tib. = Tibetan

Ajahn Chah (1918–1992) An important Thai master of the Thai Forest Tradition who had many Western disciples.

Ajahn Mun (1870–1949) A Thai master, one of the founders of the Thai Forest Tradition.

Ajahn Ranjuan A respected contemporary Thai woman meditation teacher.

Ajatasattu Son of King Bimbisara of Magadha and Queen Devi (sister of Pasenadi); after Bimbisara's abdication in his favour, King of Magadha; disciple of Devadatta.

Alara Kalama A teacher of the Buddha prior to his awakening.

Ambapali A courtesan in Vesali who became a nun at the time of the Buddha.

Ambedkar (1891–1956) A Buddhist activist, leader of India's untouchables and chief architect of the Indian Constitution.

Amitabha Buddha The Buddha responsible for the creation of the western Pure Land through the force of his forty-eight vows to save sentient beings.

Ananda First cousin of the Buddha (on his father's side); brother of Mahanama and Anuruddha; the Buddha's attendant for the last twenty-five years of his life; the monk who reputedly memorised all that the Buddha taught.

Angulimala A murderer who changed his way and became a monk after meeting the Buddha.

Anguttara Nikaya (Numerical Discourses) A compilation of Pali suttas based on numbers.

Aoyama Roshi An important Japanese Contemporary Soto Zen Abbess.

Arahant (Pal.) One who has awakened and attained nibbana through freeing oneself from greed, hatred and ignorance.

Arya Chenrezig see Chenrezig.

Ashoka (304–232 BCE) King of the Mauryan Empire in India. He propagated Buddhism across the Indian continent.

Ashvagosha (second century CE?) Author of the *Buddhacarita (Acts of the Buddha)* the first biography of the Buddha.

Assaji A disciple of the Buddha.

Assatha A type of banyan tree.

Atisha (982–1054) An Indian Master, a major figure in Tibetan Buddhism.

Atman (Skt) Literally: 'Self; in the non-Buddhist brahmanic tradition it refers to the pure consciousness that is the core of one's true being; identical in nature to Brahman (God).

Avatamsaka School A Buddhist school founded on the *Avatamsaka Sutra.*

Avatamsaka Sutra The Flower Adornment Scripture is a seminal text about the stages of the bodhisattva path and the interpenetration of all things. It has been very influential in Chinese Buddhism. It was first translated into Chinese around 420 CE.

Bhikkhu (Pal.) A fully ordained Buddhist monk. One who has left home, been fully ordained and depends on alms for a living.

Bhikkhuni (Pal.; Skt bhikshuni) A fully ordained Buddhist nun. The female counterpart of a bhikkhu.

Bimbisara King of Magadha, husband of Devi (sister of Pasenadi), father of Ajatasattu; donated the Bamboo Grove in Rajagaha to the Buddha.

Bodh Gaya A village in Central-North India where the Buddha awakened. An important place of pilgrimage for all Buddhists.

Bodhi (Pal.) Awakening.

Bodhidharma (dates uncertain; possible time of arrival in China 476 CE) The founder of the Zen school in China, a monk who came from India.

Bodhisattva (Skt; Pal. bodhisatta) One who has taken a vow to attain awakening for the sake of all sentient beings; one who aspires to become a Buddha.

Bodhisattva Precepts A list of precepts (ten major and forty-eight minor) found in the *Brahma's Net Sutra,* a Chinese Mahayanist Sutra.

Bodhi tree 'Awakening tree'. *Ficus religiosa,* pipal or assatha tree. The tree under which Sakyamuni attained enlightenment and became Buddha, situated in Bodh-Gaya, a village in Central-North India.

Brahma's Net Sutra see Bodhisattva Precepts

Brahminism Hindu religion at the time of the Buddha.

Buddha Shakyamuni The historical Buddha Gotama born about 2500 years ago in India.

Buddhabhadra (359–429) He made the first translation into Chinese of the *Flower Ornament Scripture,* a seminal text for the Chinese Buddhist traditions.

Buddhacarita Sanskrit poem of the second century CE describing the life of the Buddha.

Buddhadasa (1906–1993) An influential contemporary Thai monk.

Causality Buddhist principle of 'cause and effect': every cause has an effect, and every effect arises out of a cause.

Chaochou (778–897) A great Chinese Zen master, originator of many gongans.

Chenrezig (Tib.) Avalokitesvara (Skt) The Bodhisattva of Compassion in Mahayana Buddhism.

Chih-i (538–597) The founder of the Chinese T'ien T'ai syncretist Buddhist tradition.

Citta (Pali) Mind, can also be translated as 'heart'.

Culasunnatta Sutta A Pali sutta about voidness.

Daifukuji A Shingon temple in Japan near Nara, an ancient capital.

Deer Park A park in Sarnath near Benares where the Buddha expounded the Dhamma for the first time.

Deva (Pal.) A god; in the mundane sense, a celestial being inhabiting one of the higher realms of *samsara-*, in the supramundane sense, a Buddha who assumes a divine form in Mahayana and Vajrayana Buddhism.

Devadatta First cousin of the Buddha (on his mother's side); sought to replace the Buddha as head of the order of monks.

Dhamma (Pal.) (Skt dharma) The teaching of the Buddha; the truths and practices to which the Buddha's teaching refers.

Dhammadina A nun at the time of the Buddha whose words of wisdom have been recorded in the suttas.

Dharmagupta Vinaya The rules of discipline of the monastics of the Dharmagupta school used in China and Korea.

Dharma Nature School A Korean Buddhist School.

Diamond Vehicle see Vajrayana

Dipa APali term translated as either island or light.

Dogen (1200–1253) One of the seminal thinkers of the Soto Zen School in Japan.

Dongyu Gatsal Ling Nunnery A Tibetan Buddhist nunnery founded by Venerable Tenzin Palmo in Northern India.

Dukkha (Pal.) One of the three characteristics (impermanence, suffering and not-self). It is also translated sometimes as 'anguish' or 'stress'.

Dzogchen (Tib.) Literally: 'Great Perfection or Completion'; a formless meditation practice of pristine awareness taught in the Nyingma School of Tibetan Buddhism.

Eightfold Path Right view, right thought, right speech, right action, right livelihood right effort, right mindfulness, and right concentration.

Emperor Wu (502–550) A Chinese emperor; he met Bodhidharma.

Ficus Religiosa see Bodhi Tree

Five Aggregates The five constituents of the person: form, feeling, perception, formations, consciousness.

Five Hindrances Sensual desire, anger, laziness, restlessness, doubt.

Fokwangshan A major Buddhist temple in Taiwan.

Four Foundation of Mindfulness Body *(kaya)*, sensations *(vedana)*, mind *(citta)*, mental objects *(dhamma)*.

Four Noble Truths The noble truth of suffering, the noble truth of the origin of suffering, the noble truth of the cessation of suffering, and the noble truth of the way leading to the cessation of suffering.

Ganges One of the major Indian rivers.

Gelug School The order of Tibetan Buddhism founded by Tsongkhapa in the fifteenth century; the school in which the Dalai Lama was trained.

Going forth Leaving home to become a monk or a nun.

Gongan (Chi.; Kor. Gongan; Jap. Koan) A record of an encounter between a Zen master and a student that provokes a sudden insight; used as an object of meditation in Zen Buddhism.

Gotama see Siddhattha Gotama (can also be spelt as Gautama).

Gotami The aunt of the Buddha, his adoptive mother, and the first nun he ordained.

Guide to the Bodhisattva's Way of Life An important text in Tibetan Buddhism composed by Shantideva.

Guru Teacher in Tibetan Buddhism.

Heart Sutra An important text in Mahayana Buddhism about emptiness.

Hinayana The 'Lesser Vehicle' of Buddhism; a pejorative term coined by followers of the Mahayana to describe the supposedly 'selfish' path of the arahant in contrast to the 'altruistic' way of the bodhisattva.

Hiri (Pal.) Moral shame

Hsuan Tsang (602/603–664) An influential Chinese Buddhist monk, scholar and traveller who went to India and recorded his impressions in his autobiography.

Huiko (487–593) He is considered the Second Chinese Zen Patriarch.

Huineng (638–713) The Sixth Chinese Zen Patriarch.

Hiuwan (1913-2004) A Chinese nun who was a well-known painter, meditation master, scholar and educationalist who settled in Taiwan.

Huiyuan (334–416) He is considered the First Patriarch of the Pure Land Buddhist School.

Hungjen (601–674) The Fifth Chinese Zen Patriarch.

Hungshi (1091–1157) A Chinese Zen master who taught 'Silent illumination' meditation.

Inka In Zen, certification or authentication of one's awakening by a teacher.

Instruction for the Tenzo Important work of Dogen.

I Tsao A nun practitioner of the Pure Land tradition in Taiwan.

Jeta's Grove also Jeta Wood, an important place of practice and teaching for the Buddha and his monastics.

Jetsunma Highest honorific title for a Tibetan Buddhist nun.

Juching (1162–1228) Tsao Tung Chinese master who gave the transmission to Dogen.

Kadam School An early school of Tibetan Buddhism founded in the eleventh century by Atisha.

Kagyu School School of Tibetan Buddhism founded in the eleventh century by Marpa, Milarepa, Gompopa and their followers.

Kalinga A war won by Ashoka, the trigger for his conversion to Buddhism and peace.

Kapilavatthu The principal town of the Kosalan province of Sakya where the Buddha was raised as a child; the modern village of Piprahwa.

Karma (Skt; Pal. kamma) Literally action. Causality, the law of cause and effect.

Kassaka Sutta A short sutta about Mara (a Buddhist demon) presenting himself to the Buddha as a farmer.

Kassapa Also known as Mahakassapa (Kassapa the Great); prominent disciple of the Buddha who convened the First Council after Gotama's death.

Kaya (Pal.) Body.

Khattiya (Pali; Skt kshatriya) Indian warrior caste.

Kingdom of Wei (220–265) A Chinese empire during the three Kingdoms period.

Koliya A Sakya clan. Devadatta belonged to this clan.

Kosala The Indian kingdom to the north of the Ganges at the Buddha's time; its capital was Savatthi and its king Pasenadi.

Kuanyin (Chinese) see Chenrezig

Kukai (774–835) The founder of the Shingon (esoteric) Japanese Buddhist School.

Kumarajiva (314–413) An early and important translator of Buddhist texts into Chinese.

Kusan (1909–1983) Korean Zen master.

Lama Teacher in Tibetan Buddhism.

Licchavis At the time of the Buddha, an important clan among the clans who formed the Vajjian confederacy.

Linchi Chan School (Kor. imje; Jap. rinzai) A Chinese Zen Buddhist school using gongan as a method of meditation.

Longchen Rabjampa (1308–1364/1369?) An important teacher in the Dzogchen Tibetan Buddhist School.

Lumbini The birthplace of the Buddha, now in Nepal near the Indian border. An important pilgrimage site for Buddhists.

Madhyamaka (Skt) A Mahayana Buddhist school of thought founded on emptiness and the middle way.

Magadha The Indian kingdom to the south of the Ganges at the Buddha's time; its capital was Rajagaha and its king Bimbisara, then Ajatasattu.

Magadhi The language spoken in Magadha.

Maggasamyutta Sutta A sutta about the analysis of the path, contained in the *Connected Discourses*.

Mahamangala Sutta A short text about protection. It is contained in the *Sutta Nipata* discourses.

Mahapajapati see Gotami.

Maha-parinibbana Sutta An important sutta featuring the last days of the Buddha. It is found in the *Collection of Long Discourses.*

Mahasanghika An early (more liberal) Buddhist school no longer in existence; it arose after the Council of Vesali.

Mahavira (fifth century BCE) Contemporary of the Buddha, an important figure in Jainism, an Indian religion based on non-violence.

Mahayana The 'Greater Vehicle' of Buddhism, which encourages the bodhisattva's aspiration to become a Buddha for the sake of all beings.

Mandala A complex three-dimensional image used in visualisation in tantric meditation.

Mantra An incantation; a mystical formula usually composed of Sanskrit syllables. It is often associated with a particular Buddha or Bodhisattva and is recited in a continuous and repetitive manner.

Marpa The teacher of Milarepa, founding figure of the Tibetan Kagyu School.

Maurya dynasty (321–185 BCE) Founded by Chandragupta, extended by his grandson Ashoka.

Maya The name traditionally given to the mother of the Buddha. She is believed to have died shortly after giving birth.

Milarepa (1028/40?–1111/23?) An esteemed teacher in the Tibetan tradition and considered one of the founders of the Kagyu School.

Milinda (Greek: Menander) He reigned in the second century BCE over an Indo-Greek kingdom in Northwest India.

Milindapanha Question of King Milinda Discussion between an Indo-Greek king and a Buddhist monk called Nagasena found in the Pali canon.

Mindfulness Paying attention to one's inner and outer conditions and experiences with a calm and alert awareness.

Mindfulness-Based Cognitive Therapy A therapy combining mindfulness and cognitive therapy to help people who have suffered several occurrences of depression.

Mitta A Sakyan woman, one of the first nuns at the time of the Buddha. She is mentioned in *Psalms of the Nuns (Therigatha).*

Moggallana With Sariputta, one of the two senior disciples of the Buddha; he was a brahmin from Magadha and became renowned for his meditative and psychic powers.

Mudra The symbolic hand gestures of figures, such as the Buddha, depicted in iconographic statues and paintings.

Muni A sage or one who is silent.

Nagarjuna (around second century CE) An important philosopher in the Mahayana tradition.

Nagasena A Buddhist monk of the second century BCE who had a remarkable dialogue with King Milinda.

Nalanda An Ancient Buddhist University situated in Bihar, India. It was destroyed in 1197 by a Muslim invasion of Northern India. The Chinese Buddhist pilgrim Hsuan Tsang visited it in the seventh century.

Nanda A half-brother of the Buddha who became a monk and who had difficulty adapting to the renunciant life.

Nibbana (Pal.; Skt nirvana) The 'blowing out' of the 'fires' of greed, hatred and ignorance. The quiescent state realised though the cessation of suffering, delusion and craving. It also refers to the passing away of the Buddha, as in 'after the nirvana of the Buddha'.

Nyingma School The 'Ancient' school of Tibetan Buddhism founded in the 8th century during the first phase of the dissemination of Buddhism in Tibet.

Ottapa (Pal.) Moral dread.

Pabhassara Sutta An extremely short sutta found in the *Numerical Discourses* which describes the mind as luminous.

Padmasambhava (eighth or ninth century?) An Indian sage who is considered the founder of Tibetan tantric Buddhism.

Pali The Middle Indo-Aryan language used to record the Buddha's teaching as found in the canonical literature of the Theravada school.

Pali Canon The original Buddhist scriptures. The canonical literature of the Theravada school.

Paramitas 'perfections'. Qualities to cultivate on the path of awakening. Often six are mentioned: generosity, morality, patience, effort, concentration and wisdom.

Paranibbana Synonym of nibbana, often refering to the final passing away of the Buddha.

Pasenadi King of Kosala during the Buddha's lifetime.

Patimokkha Code of discipline: in general, it refers to a certain number of commandments for monks and for nuns as found in the Vinaya texts. They should be read in assembly twice a month, at which time each monk or nun is invited to confess any violations.

Pavarana Monastic ceremony of mutual confession. It generally happens at the end of the rains retreat.

Perfection of Wisdom Class of Buddhist Mahayana literature.

Perfect One One of the names given to the Buddha; others are 'Blessed One', 'Lord', etc.

Platform Sutra An important sutra for the Zen tradition. It is the life and teaching of the Sixth Chinese Zen Patriarch, Hui Neng. It has been incorporated in the Mahayana Chinese Buddhist Canon.

Prakrits Name given to colloquial languages existing at the time of the Buddha.

Pure Land In Mahayana Buddhism, a realm created by the compassion of a Bodhisattva or a Buddha.

Rahula Son of the Buddha; he became a monk himself at an early age.

Rain retreat Three-month traditional monastic retreat which happens during the raining season (mid-July to mid-October) in Southeast Asia.

Rajagaha Capital city of Magadha; the modern town of Rajgir.

Rohini river The name of a river that flowed between two Sakya clans, the Gotamas and the Koliyas.

Rupa (Skt, Pali) form, corporeality. One of the five aggregates.

Saicho (767–822) The founder of the Tendai School in Japan.

Sakya (the land of) Eastern province of the kingdom of Kosala where the Buddha was born; its capital was Kapilavatthu.

Sakyamuni see Buddha Sakyamuni.

Sakya School A school of Tibetan Buddhism, named after the region in Southern Tibet where its founding teachers originated in the eleventh century.

Samatha (Pal.) 'mental calm', a concentrated equanimous state of mind.

Samma (Pal.) Right, correct, just, total, whole, real, authentic.

Sampajanna (Pal.) Clear apprehension of oneself in all aspects of the moment.

Samsara (Pal.) The painful and repetitive cycle of death and rebirth.

Sangha (Pal.) 'Community'. The community of people committed to the practice of Dhamma, sometimes used exclusively to refer to ordained monks and nuns.

Sanghamitta A Buddhist nun, the daughter of King Ashoka who brought Buddhism to Sri Lanka.

Sanjaya A teacher of Moggallana and Sariputta who upheld an agnostic position.

Sankhara (Pal.) Literally 'that which has been put together'. Complex Pali term, often translated as 'mental formation' or 'volition'.

Sariputta With Moggallana, one of the two senior disciples of the Buddha; he was a brahmin from Magadha and was renowned for his intelligence and wisdom.

Sarnath Deer Park where the Buddha first taught the Dhamma.

Sati (Pal.) Memory or recognition. It is also used as intentness of mind, wakefulness, mindfulness, awareness, alertness, or lucidity.

Satipatthana Sutta The *Foundations of Mindfulness Discourse*, which can be found in the *Middle Length Sayings*.

Satisampajanna Recollection and clear comprehension, mindfulness and lucidity.

Savatthi Capital city of the kingdom of Kosala; the Jeta's Grove was nearby; the modern town of Sahet Mahet/Sravasti.

Sengtsan Third Chinese Zen Patriarch.

Seven Factors of Enlightenment Mindfulness, investigation of the Dhamma, energy, joy, calm, concentration, equanimity.

Shantideva Eighth-century Indian Mahayana Buddhist monk; author of A *Guide to the Bodhisattva's Way of Life (Bodhicaryavatara)*.

Shao Lin Temple Buddhist temple near Loyang in China connected to Bodhidharma and kung fu.

Shikantaza 'Just sitting'; Japanese-style Zen meditation.

Shingon The tantric or esoteric school of Japanese Buddhism.

Shobogenzo Treasury of the True Dartna Eye Important work written by Dogen.

Shunyata Literally emptiness. The absence of inherent existence in persons or things.

Siddhattha Gotama (Pal.) Personal name of the Buddha, the 'Awakened One'.

Sigala Young man to whom the Buddha taught the *Sigalovada Sutta* or lay discipline.

Sigalovada Sutta Also known as the *Sigalaka Sutta.* It is found in the *Collection of Long Discourses.*

Six bases These are the six sense bases: eyes, ears, tongues, nose, body and consciousness.

Sona A monk at the time of the Buddha

Songgwangsa Temple Korean Buddhist Zen temple where Master Kusan and the author resided.

Songtsen Gampo (605/617?–649) Tibetan King, traditionally credited with establishing Buddhism in Tibet.

Soto Zen (Jap.; Chi. Tsao Tung) A school of Zen Buddhism founded in China.

Sravasti Buddhist Temple Temple of Ven. Thubten Chodron in Washington State.

Sthaviras The Elders, the name of a Buddhist group that developed after the time of the Buddha

Suddhodana (Pali) The Buddha's father.

Sumedho Contemporary Western monk, important disciple of Ajahn Chah.

Sutta (Pal; Skt sutra) A discourse delivered by the Buddha or, on occasion, one of his prominent disciples.

Ta Hui (1089–1163) Important Chinese Zen Master.

Tairyu Elderly Japanese nun of the Shingon tradition.

Tantra An esoteric path to enlightenment using mantra, transformative imagination and yogic exercises.

Taohsin (580–651) Fourth Chinese Zen Patriarch.

Tathagata 'Thus come or thus gone'. One of the ten traditional epithets given to the Buddha, who often referred to himself by this name.

Tendai School (Jap.) A syncretist sixth-century school of Chinese Buddhism founded by Chih-I, which subsequently developed in Japan.

Ten precepts For monastics: refraining from killing, stealing, any sexual behaviour, taking any intoxicants, eating at the wrong time, singing or dancing, or attending performances, wearing perfumes or cosmetics, sitting on high chairs or sleeping on high beds, accepting money.

Tenzin Palmo Contemporary revered English Buddhist Tibetan nun.

Theravada Literally 'The Teaching of the Elders'. The school of Buddhism found today in Sri Lanka and Southeast Asia that is based on the Pali Canon and the commentaries of Buddhaghosa.

Therigatha (*Verses* or *Psalms of the Nuns*), a collection of seventy-three poems from nuns from the time of the Buddha.

Three fires/three poisons Greed, hatred and ignorance.

Three trainings Ethics, meditation and wisdom.

T'ien T'ai School A syncretist sixth-century school of Chinese Buddhism founded by Chih-I.

Toui (d.825) First significant Korean Zen teacher.

Triple Gems or **Three Jewels** Buddha, Dharma and Sangha.

Triple Refuge Taking refuge in the Triple Gems. This often takes place during lay or monastic ordination ceremonies.

Tubten Chodron An American Gelugpa nun from the Tibetan tradition. Born in 1950, she became a nun in 1977, and an influential teacher in the USA.

Uddaka Ramaputta An Indian teacher of the Buddha prior to his awakening.

Upali The monk who recited the Vinaya texts after the death of the Buddha.

Upanishads (Skt) A class of non-Buddhist religious-philosophical literature that explores the ways to achieve union with Brahman (God); also known as Vedanta, i.e. the 'end' or 'culmination' of the Vedas.

Uposatha A fast-day. Also refers to the bi-monthly ceremony during which the recitation of the patimokkha happens after the monks or nuns have confessed to each other.

Vairocana Buddha The name of a Buddha; according to the Avatamsaka Sutra, the Buddha whose body is said symbolically to constitute the universe.

Vajjian Confederacy The last surviving republic of the Buddha's time, located to the north of the Ganges and south of Malla; its capital city was Vesali.

Vajrayana 'Diamond Vehicle'. The path of tantric Buddhism, which emerged in India from approximately the third century CE; involves the use of mantra, visualisation and yogic exercises; it is widely practised in all schools of Tibetan Buddhism.

Vassa see rain retreat.

Vedana (Pal.) Mental or bodily sensations, feeling-tones, as in pleasant, unpleasant and neither-pleasant-nor-unpleasant feeling-tones.

Veda A class of Brahmanic, non-Buddhist religious literature, consisting mainly of hymns to the gods; the earliest expression of Aryan culture in India prior to the Upanishads.

Verses from the Center An essential work of Nagarjuna.

Vesali Capital city of Vajji; the modern village of Vaishali.

Vidudhaba Son of King Pasenadi and Vasabha; briefly ruled as king of Kosala after the overthrow of Pasenadi.

Vinaya Literally 'discipline'. The moral rules and codes of conduct of Buddhist monks and nuns; the body of literature in the Pali Canon that describes monastic life and practice.

Vipassana Literally 'penetrative insight'. A Buddhist meditation that is concerned with investigating the nature of experience.

Vulture Peak Small hill situated above Rajagaha where the Buddha liked to meditate and is reputed to have given some Mahayana teachings.

Vyaggapajja Sutta A text about ethics found in the *Numerical Discourses.*

Wat Bah Pong A temple in Thailand, belonging to the Forest Tradition, founded by Ajahn Chah.

Wat Nanachat A temple in Thailand for Western monastics founded by Ajahn Chah.

Wonhyo (617–686 CE) An original thinker and the founder of the Dharma Nature School in Korea.

Zazen Literally 'sitting meditation'. According to the Sixth Zen Patriarch: 'where the mind has nowhere to abide'.

Zen (Jap.; Chi. Chan; Kor. Seon) A meditative form of Buddhism that originated in sixth-century China and spread to Korea and Japan.

Bibliography

Page numbers in square brackets refer to quotations in the present volume

MOST QUOTATIONS ARE TAKEN FROM THE FOLLOWING:

The Life of the Buddha, as it appears in the Pali Canon, ed. and trans. Bhikkhu Nanamoli, Buddhist Publication Society, Sri Lanka, 1978.
Other translated quotations from the Pali Canon are taken from the following:
Anguttara Nikaya, Numerical Discourses, ed. and trans. Nyanaponika Thera and Bhikkhu Bodhi, AltaMira, Walnut Creek CA, 1999. [pp. 14, 43, 65, 79, 90, 91, 92, 98 (twice), 99, 115]
Dhammapada, trans. Acharya Buddharakkhita, Buddhist Publication Society, Sri Lanka, 1985. [p. 114]
Digha Nikaya – The Long Discourses of the Buddha, trans. Maurice Walshe, Wisdom Publications, Boston, 1987. [pp. 32, 36, 38, 39, 40, 41, 72, 77, 82, 100, 121]
Majjhima Nikaya – The Middle Length Discourses of the Buddha: A New translation of the Majjhima Nikaya (Teachings of the Buddha), trans. Bhikkhu Nanamoli and ed. Bhikkhu Bodhi, Wisdom Publications, Boston, 1995. [pp. 59, 61, 69, 75, 76, 84, 85]

Milindapanha – Questions of King Milinda, trans. T.W. Rhys Davids, *Sacred Books of the East,* vols XXXV and XXXVI, Clarendon/Oxford, 1890–4; reprinted by Motilal Banarsidass, Delhi, [p. 123]

Therigatha – The First Buddhist Women: Translations and Commentary on the Therigatha, trans, and ed. Susan Murcott, Parallax Press, Berkeley, 1991.

Udana, trans. John D. Ireland, Buddhist Publication Society, Sri Lanka, 1997. [pp. 14, 62, 80, 94, 106]

The poem on page ix is a private translation by Andrew Olendzki.

The quotation from the *Digha Nikaya* on p. 27 is by Stephen Batchelor.

QUOTATIONS IN CHAPTER 9 AND 10 ARE TAKEN FROM THE FOLLOWING:

The Heart of the Perfection of Wisdom Sutra, trans. Robert Buswell, private papers. [p. 122]

Verses from the Center, Stephen Batchelor, Riverhead Books, New York 2000. [pp. 124, 125, 136]

The Flower Ornament Scripture – The Avatamsaka Sutra, Thomas Cleary, Shambhala, Boston 1984. [p. 125]

The Chinese Bodhisattva Precepts – Brahma's Net Sutra, trans. Martine Batchelor, AltaMira, California, 2004. [p. 127]

The Blue Cliff Record, trans. Thomas Geary, Shambhala, Boston. 1977. [p. 129]

The Platform Sutra of the Sixth Patriarch, trans. Philip B. Yampolski, Columbia University Press, New York, 1967. [p. 130]

On Cultivating Determination to Practise, trans. Samu Sunim and Martine Batchelor, private papers, [p. 131]

Quotation of Geshe Gonpapa, in *Essential Advice of the Kadampa Masters,* trans. Lama Geshe Wangyal, in *The Jewel in the Lotus,* ed. Stephen Batchelor, Visdom Publications, Boston, 1987. [p. 132]

A Guide to the Bodhisattva's Way of Life, Shantideva, trans. Stephen Batchelor, Library of Tibetan Works and Archives, Dharamsala, 1979. [p. 134]

Quotation from Milarepa, in *The Jewel in the Lotus,* ed. Stephen Batchelor, Wisdom Publications, Boston, 1987. [p. 135]

Swampland Flowers: The letters and Lectures of Zen Master Ta Hui, J.C. Cleary, Shambhala, Boston, 2006. [pp. 129, 130]

Cultivating the Empty Field: The Silent Illumination of Zen Master Hongzhi, Taigen Daniel Leighton (trans.) with Yi Wu, North Point Press, California, 1991. [p. 138]

Quotation from Longchen Rabjampa, in *The Jewel in the Lotus,* ed. Stephen Batchelor, Wisdom Publications, Boston, 1987. [p. 139]

Moon in a Dewdrop: Writings of Zen Master Dogen, ed. Tanahashi Kazuaki, North Point Press, Berkeley and Element Books, Shaftesbury, Dorset, 1988. [p. 141]

Bodhinyana, Ajahn Chah, Chuan Printing Press, Bangkok, 1979. [p. 145]

Quotation from Ajahn Ranjuan, in *Women's Buddhism, Buddhism's Wonen*, ed. Ellison Banks Findly, Wisdom Publications, Boston, 2000. [p. 146]

Dr Amhedkar, Buddhism and Social Change, A.K. Narain and D.C. Ahir; B.R. Publishing Corporation, India, 1994. [p. 147]

Reflections on a Mountain Lake, Tenzin Palmo, Snow Lion Publications, Ithaca, 2002. [p. 148]

Open Heart, Clear Mind, Thubten Chodron, Snow Lion, Ithaca, New York, 1990. [p. 149]

Zen Seeds, Aoyama Shundo, Kosei Publishing, Tokyo, 1990. [p. 151]

Quotation from Itsao Fashih, in *Walking on Lotus Flowers: Buddhist Women Living, Loving and Meditating*, Martine Batchelor, Thorsons, London, 1996. [p. 152]

Ven. Eko S. Noble, private interview with Martine Batchelor, 1992. [p. 153]

Quotation from Shig Hiu Wan, in *Walking on Lotus Flowers: Buddhist Women Living Loving and Meditating*, Martine Batchelor, Thorsons, London, 1996. [p. 154]

Quotation from Darlene Cohen, in *Being Bodies*, ed. Lenore Friedman and Suisan Moon, Shambhala, Boston, 1997. [p. 155]

The Engaged Spiritual Life, Donald Rothberg, Beacon Press, Boston, 2006. [p, 155]

Mindfulness-Based Cognitive Therapy for Depression, Zindel V. Segal, Mark G. Williams, and John D. Teasdale, The Guilford Press, New York, 2002. [p. 156]

SCHOLARLY TEXTS CONSULTED AND MENTIONED

H. Bechert and R. Gombrich, ed., *The World of Buddhism*, Thames & Hudson, London, 1984.

R.E. Buswell, jr., editor in chief, *Encyclopedia of Buddhism*, Thomson Gale – Macmillan Reference, USA, 2004.

E. Conze, *A Short History of Buddhism*, George Allen & Unwin, London, 1980.

R.F. Gombrich, *How Buddhism Began*, Athlone, London, 1996.

H. Nakamura, *Gotama Buddha*, Buddhist Books International, Los Angeles – Tokyo, 1977.

H.W. Schumann, *The Historical Buddha*, Motilal Banarsidas, Delhi, 2004 (reprint).

RECOMMENDED BOOKS

Batchelor, Martine, Principles of Zen, Thorsons, London, 1999.

Batchelor, Stephen, The Awakening of the West: The Encounter of Buddhism and Western Culture, Parallax Press, Berkeley, 1995.

Buswell, Robert E., jr., trans., Tracing back the Radiance, University of Hawaii Press, 1991.

Chah, Ajahn, A Taste of Freedom: Selected Dhamma Talks, Vipassana Research Publications, 1988.

Dalai Lama, Ethics for the New Millennium, Riverhead Books, New York, 1999.

Goldstein, Joseph, Insight Meditation: The Practice of Freedom, Shambhala, Boston, 1994.

Mackenzie, Vicki, Cave in the Snow: Tenzin Palmo's Quest for Enlightenment, Bloomsbury, London, 1998.

Queen, Christopher S., and King Sallie B., (ed.), Engaged Buddhism: Buddhist Liberation Movements in Asia, State University of New York Press, Albany, 1996.

Rabten, Geshe, and Dargyey, Geshe, Advice from a Spiritual Friend, Wisdom Publications, Boston, 1986.

Salzberg, Sharon, Loving-Kindness: The Revolutionary Art of Happiness, Shambhala, Boston, 1997.

Sengstan, Hsin Hsin Ming: Verses on the Faith Mind, trans. Richard B. Clarke, New York, 1976.